the Sport of Learning™

A Comprehensive Survival Guide for African-American Student-Athletes

Vince Fudzie, Andre Hayes, and the Boyz
Co-authored by Student-Athletes for Student-Athletes

PUBLISHED BY
DOUBLEPLAY PUBLISHING GROUP

The Sport of Learning

For information contact: Doubleplay Publishing Group
P.O. Box 5396
North Hollywood, CA 91616
510-886-2415

Library of Congress Cataloging-in-Publication Data
Fudzie, Vince.
      The Sport of Learning / Vince Fudzie and Andre N. Hayes

      Includes index.
      ISBN 0-9652824-0-6 (pbk)
      1. School sports—United States. 2. Athletes—United States. 3. High School sports—United States.
      4. College Sports—United States. 5. College athletes—United States. 6. African American
      athletes—United States. I. Hayes, Andre. II. Title.

The *Sport of Learning* is available at special discounts when purchased in bulk quantities for schools, teams, associations, institutions or sales promotions. Please contact the Special Sales Department at 510-886-2415.

Text & Cover Design by: Sabrina Meyers *(i d e e* Design; Ypsilanti, Michigan)
Photography by: Peter Yates
Editing by: Andrea Perry
Student-Athletes on cover (left-right): Korye Jones, Yusef Dibble, Rodney Gray

Printed in the United States of America.

This book is printed on acid-free paper.

Acknowledgments

Our Creator Above

Joan Johnson
Richard Lapchick
Gladys Hayes
Robert Sellers
Lulu Hayes
Ken Shropshire
Monique "MoMo" Ware
Livia Hansbro
Art Tiel
Fred Whitfield
Erica Lewis
Danielle Williams
Edward Davis
John Ross

Leslie Wise
Ariana Fudzie
Dewayne Fuqua
Tracey Revis-Hayes
Brenda Taylor
Tracy Allen
Denise McFarland
Guillermo Rubio
Wil Jacobs
Falita Knight
Norwaine Reed
Travor Hill
Akkida McDowell
Estina Thompson

All of our boys at the following schools:

University of California, Berkeley
University of Southern California
University of California, Los Angeles
University of Texas, Austin
University of Nebraska
University of Michigan
University of N. Carolina, Chapel Hill
University, Arizona State
University of Washington
University, Eastern Michigan

And anyone else who assisted, prayed, wished, or pushed for the successful completion of this project which has been long overdue. WAY TO LOOK OUT.

IN EVERYTHING SET THEM AN EXAMPLE BY DOING WHAT IS GOOD. IN YOUR TEACHING SHOW INTEGRITY, SERIOUSNESS AND SOUNDNESS OF SPEECH THAT CANNOT BE CONDEMNED, SO THAT THOSE WHO OPPOSE YOU MAY BE ASHAMED BECAUSE THEY HAVE NOTHING BAD TO SAY ABOUT US.
—Titus 2: 7-8 NIV

Please Note: The views expressed throughout this guide solely represent those of the primary authors and of the numerous contributing present and former student-athletes. Chapters written by other individuals are deemed to be the views of said individuals, with the blessings of the primary authors. Please be advised that the authors are not mental or physical health care practitioners, and so you should consult a competent health care provider on serious issues relating to mental or physical health. The authors are merely young brothers who made it successfully through a system where success has been historically difficult to obtain. In all cases, we believe the material is presented in a way which achieves the maximum impact of disseminating information to our target audience. The chief aim of the material is to increase the graduation rate among student-athletes and hopefully to assist in the development of young people in the process.

Table of Contents

FRONT COURT

by Richard E. Lapchick, Diretor of the Center for the Study of Sports in Society, Northeastern University, Boston, Massachusetts

The Sport of Learning is long overdue and will be a guide for African-American male student-athletes to better move through the maze of all the pressures associated with athletics, of all the illusions surrounding athletics, and the realities of athletics in America.

For those of you who are student-athletes, Vince Fudzie and Andre Hayes have made a major contribution to enhance your possibilities for success in the future. I know Andre and Vince have made this a passion of love to help the next generation avoid some of the pitfalls that have trapped so many of the current generation of student-athletes.

The book focuses on African-American male student-athletes as those who are most heavily recruited to play football and basketball in the country. Among African-American males and females and white males and females, African-American males have the lowest graduation rate. The purpose of the book seems clear. The authors present a sequence of events from high school through the college years that are realistic, in the language of young people in the 1990's, and convey a simple message. If you are more aware of where you are going, you will get there more successfully.

The topics covered in the book as well as the contributors to the book are all inclusive. The book is a must read for both student-athletes and their parents. It has a base that does not overlook the history of African-Americans, both in sport and in our society. There are insights from coaches of the highest caliber. There are realistic methods given to help high school student-athletes realize which factors should go into their decision on which college to choose. They also help prepare high school student-athletes for what will be required to be eligible in college, including all the new academic standards that have been passed by the NCAA. It raises the all important questions of what is going to happen to African-American student-athletes who suddenly finds themselves on a college campus that is overwhelmingly white, both in the student body, the faculty and the surrounding area of the campus.

The book will help student-athletes and give insights to their parents on how they can support them when they are in college, balancing academics and athletics. It provides study skills and time management plans. **The Sport of Learning** shows ways to talk to coaches and academic officials that will express both how you feel, yet not alienate those people so that they will become your supporters.

Many African-American student-athletes arrive on our campuses without the possibility of financial support from home. Yet, according to NCAA rules, they are not able to work during the academic year. Fudzie and Hayes provide realistic approaches to managing your money while you are in college so that you are not tempted to compromise your integrity and the integrity of the entire athletic program.

The book also presents, in graphic detail, the sexual issues on our campuses today from sexually transmitted diseases to the overwhelming issue of gender violence. Athletes coming to our campuses should know that there is a major stereotype out there and that athletes, particularly African-American athletes, are more inclined to be gender violent. This is believed by white coeds, white policeman and the white media. There is no study that has ever been published that shows this to be the case. In fact, the data compiled by Northeastern University' s Center for the Study of Sport in Society shows exactly the opposite. Yet because of those stereotypes, the chapters on relationships with college co-eds on your new campus is critical information. It also talks in detail, and in depth, about substance abuse and how it can be another trap to block your goals.

The book discusses dealing with the media, a media that is overwhelmingly white. With 1,600 daily newspapers in America, as of this writing, there are only two African-American sports editors in major media markets and only 11 African-American columnists; 90% of the 1,600 daily newspapers in America don't have a single African-American sports writer. So you have to be prepared to work with a group of reporters during your college careers who may not understand you or your culture. The media relations chapter will be critical for how you deal with this.

If you make it far enough that you are being considered to be a professional athlete, the chapter on how to handle or avoid agents will be critical to getting the right agent. You could lose your eligibility because of an illegal act by an agent while you are in school. This is going to be very important for those who reach that highest level in the later years of their college careers.

Finally, the chapter on African—American culture and its relevance to everyday society draws from historical African-American leaders who can help you put yourself in the context of the culture that you live in.

Now that you have this incredible resource in **The Sport of Learning**, I wish you all the best in your remaining career in high school, future and potential future careers in college as a student-athlete, and the pros, if you should make it.

To the parents, I hope you can enjoy your son's academic and athletic achievements and encourage him in both areas. He is a gifted person in a society that values athletics for Africans Americans more than academics. Its up to all of you to make sure that your son maintains the balance between any dreams of an athletic career with the reality of getting a sound academic base so he can be prepared to have a successful life, be it in sports or not. **The Sport of Learning** will help you to do that.

MANHOOD: Toward A Definition

by Dr. T. Garrott Benjamin, Jr.

One of the greatest challenges facing the African-American male population today is how to make the successful transition from boys to men. In the African culture, the attainment of manhood was clearly defined by a regimented process called the "rite of passage." African boys were systematically carried through tests of spiritual development, physical strength, character, responsibility, and integrity to provide them with the foundations to become strong men. Each step was clearly marked along the way and culminated with a feast formally welcoming the boy into manhood.

Having had their connection to the Motherland severed, our African-American boys often find their definition of manhood in the warped reality of gangs, drugs, alcohol, premarital sex, low academic performance, prison, or violent death at the hands of a society out of control. Thus, the definition of manhood for many of our African-American boys has been misconstrued to the point that it actually destroys the Black male child rather than building him up.

The essence of true manhood is not found in externals traits: physical strength, money, or possessions. It is found in internal traits: character, values, and integrity. Manhood carries with it the personal characteristics of self-respect, respect for others, courage, responsibility, duty, honor, steadfastness, and morality. The essence of manhood is presenting one's personal best at all times. It is found in a willingness to work hard. Manhood is found in being responsible and responsive to the needs of others. It is found in realizing that you don't have to be "a remarkable person to do remarkable things."

Manhood at best is a spiritual journey that allows a process of growth where a man spends his life seeking to become like his Creator. The Apostle Paul said it best when he pointed to his transition from boyhood to manhood. He said, "When I was a child, I spoke like a child; I understood like a child; I thought like a child. When I became a man, I threw away childish things." Manhood is a transition that every boy must make. It will take responsible men to help boys make that transition. Manhood begins when a man reaches back and helps a boy. The real "rite of passage" is when a father becomes both a model and a mentor to his son. Nobody can teach a boy to be a man but a man. It is up to all of us to break the cycle of pain by taking responsibility in helping boys to become men. *This* is the true essence of manhood.

COACHES' CORNER

A candid round table discussion with highly respected coaches on their perception of the problems facing today's African American student-athlete and what can be done to solve these problems.

John Chaney, Temple University basketball coach
Don James, University of Washington football coach (retired)
George Raveling, University of Southern California basketball coach (retired)

Andre: What do you perceive as the problem with today's African American student-athlete?

Coach Raveling: I think that what all student athletes need to do, and in particular African-American student-athletes, is to gain a balanced perspective. In essence, they need to have an equal appreciation of the academic side of college life, as they do for the athletic side. Too often because of the people exterior of them, their perspective is more focused on the athletics than it is on the social and the academic side.

Coach James: Most people enjoy doing what they do or are prepared to do best. Any student athlete that enrolls in a university and is not as prepared as the average students at that school, will in all likelihood experience problems. In my opinion, it is like going into an athletic contest as the underdog. This is the result of a lack of preparation at the lower levels.

Coach Chaney: As I see it, the problem with today's African-American student-athletes in particular, is that they don't listen to advice from their elders. We often speak to kids in terms of "when I was coming up…" Today's student-athletes don't want to hear that, and they can't listen because they are to busy talking. They also are growing up to today with poor role models. Too much emphasis is put on becoming a professional athlete, and today these kids come in with the wrong attitude.

Andre: What can institutions do to resolve the problem?

Coach Raveling: Well, I think that it's never too late to try to help young people grow into responsible adults. At the college level, one of the things the institutions could do is to work with the student-athletes in the area of people skills. In the coming decade, the people who are going to be the most successful are those who have developed the best people skills.

Coach James: Both the institution and the individual must be motivated to spend additional time to play catch up. Colleges need a quality counseling/mentoring and tutorial program. The student athlete needs help and must be willing to put in additional hours in preparation for each of their courses. Coaches must also see to it that the student-athletes have the time to study, and insist that they participate in tutoring programs.

Coach Chaney: In order to reach student-athletes, schools have to develop clear and succinct goals that have a gradual progression attached. Often times the emphasis is on some distant reward in the future, and kids don't want to hear that. There is a need to systematically put a method into place which offers a constant re-stating and re-evaluating of a student-athletes' goals. This would keep them on the road to academic and career success, while satisfying their need to see immediate accomplishments and rewards. There is nothing wrong with wanting to achieve pro status, but they need to understand the odds and develop career alternatives with the same passion they use to develop their athletic skills.

Andre: What advice would you give to the parents of student-athletes?

Coach Raveling: First of all, I think that one of the fundamental missions of parents is to help their children see the best in themselves. Parents have to help their children realize their potential as student-athletes and as human beings. Parents need to build a strong value system in their children that they can take with them as they move into the adult world.

Coach James: I would advise parents of the necessity to do a better job in the early years of education. Elementary and middle school years are critical to the total developmental process. Our parents, teachers and counselors must be more positive and should encourage youngsters to do well in school via positive reinforcement, rather than telling them that they cannot make it. Parents and teachers must challenge their students to do their best. Sending the colleges better student-athletes will increase graduation.

Coach Chaney: My advice to parents is simple. Don't focus on the non-sense about family values and single parents being the cause of our nations problems. Single parents did not just evolve in the 1990's, and I know of many single parents who have successfully raised their kids. Don't turn your kids off by focusing on what you did "back in your day". Steer them towards good role models or, better yet, be that role model. The extended family is crucial for their development and supervision. These points are only the tip of the iceberg, but they are a good start.

Andre: We would like to thank you gentlemen for your time and participation in this segment of the book.

HOW TO USE THIS PLAYBOOK

Getting Started

- Use the Table of Contents or Index to identify your area of interest.

- Each chapter is self-contained, so you can read the chapters in the order that suits you.

- Chapters include worksheets, self-tests and sample scenarios. Feel free to write out responses as you would in a workbook, in order to get the maximum benefit.

- *The Sport of Learning* is not intended to be a detailed analysis of every possible situation, but rather a means to heighten your awareness. In doing so, it is our hope that it will help you use good judgment in your daily decisions.

- While reading, keep in mind that you personally possess the skills and strengths to be successful both academically and athletically. *The Sport of Learning* gives you direction on how to best use your skills and strengths in everyday life.

The Sport of Learning is easy reading, written by individuals who have been where you are trying to go. You will not only find it enjoyable, but more importantly, beneficial to you as a guidebook for success in life. Get acquainted with it, and you can probably read it in a couple of days, no sweat.

We hope that you will find as much promise and fulfillment in reading *The Sport of Learning* as we did in putting it together.

How to get the most out of The Sport of Learning

The Sport of Learning is written for you, the student-athlete from middle school to college. Although many of the topics discussed are addressed from the perspective of the college student-athlete, the principles and lessons taught are applicable to all student-athletes. So take what is offered, and apply it to your own situation.

Dexter Manley had it all.

He vaulted to stardom as a player for the Oklahoma State University football team, then kicked ass for the Washington Redskins as an all-pro defensive end.

Hero. Millionaire. Star athlete. Super Bowl veteran.

Dexter Manley could lay claim to all of those titles. *What he could not lay claim to was being a well educated man.*

Despite having graduated from Houston, Texas's public schools and attending a four-year college, Dexter could not read or write. He finally did something about it at the age of twenty-seven, when he entered Washington, D.C.'s Lab School. That's where he was diagnosed as having an auditory channel problem that made it difficult for him to remember what he heard. He was reading at a second grade level.

Apparently, not one single teacher in the Houston school system or professor at Oklahoma State knew that Dexter could not read or write. Nor, evidently, did any of his coaches.

No matter. Whether Dexter could read and write had no impact on his significant achievements in football. But his achievements certainly had an impact on the sport—especially in terms of dollars. Dexter took home some serious cash over the years, but during his stellar career, he yielded untold millions for the sports industry. From the fans who packed the stands at high school football games to those who crowded into million-dollar arenas, people paid big bucks to watch Dexter at work. The sports industry as a whole, from team owners and agents to T-shirt hawkers and concessionaires, pocketed more of those dollars than Dexter ever did.

Even worse, by the time Dexter's playing days ended, his personal troubles were rapidly accelerating.

The Dexter Manley story is a sad one. It also fills us with rage. We know, and so do you, that what happened to Dexter is not an exception. Today, there are many young brothers too preoccupied with dreams of a career in some league to concentrate on school. A recent Louis Harris survey shows that **thirty-two percent** of all high school male football and basketball players think they will play professionally. Even more staggering is that **forty-three percent** of all African-American student-athletes think they can make the pros.

These fellas spend their days dribbling, passing, blocking, or dunking their way to a fantasy career in some league. When it comes to sports, they dream big. When it comes to school, they dream of ways to avoid the drudgery of readin', writin', and 'rithmetic. After all, they won't need those skills: when they make the pros, and sign all those endorsements, and make that first mil, somebody else will sweat all that other stuff. That's the dream.

The reality is that, for the lucky few who beat the odds, their careers will average about three years, which means they'll be retired at an early age. Who knows whether they will have any money left for their "golden years." And it's a safe bet that they won't have a college degree to help them launch a second career. How do we know? Personal experience. We have seen too many of our friends who failed to receive an adequate education, and the turn their lives took once they were out of the sports limelight. Studies indicate that **fewer than forty percent** of minority student-athletes at the college level actually graduate; even fewer receive more than a basic education. We also know that, even

Many people want to know why this book targets African-American male student-athletes. They argue that problems such as low graduation rates and illiteracy affect all athletes. We don't deny that. Our concern is that these problems occur at a more alarming rate for *African-American male* student-athletes. Males of other races fare better. Women, including African-Americans, fare better. Obviously, somebody needs to focus attention on African-American male student-athletes.

though every student is ultimately responsible for his own academic success, the college athletic environment plays a role in his success or failure. For various reasons this environment, simply put, is not always conducive to learning.

As two African-American men and former student-athletes who succeeded at rising above our disadvantaged upbringing, we are now dedicated to offering direction to young brothers. We have co-founded the *African-American Athletic Alumni Association*, a nonprofit organization designed to increase the graduation rate of minority student-athletes. And, of course, we have written this book, in which we share the insights and experiences of former student-athletes, as well as our own.

Our hearts go out to people like Dexter Manley. Still, we are tired of student-athletes who sacrifice all for sports and nothing for an education. We are livid over schools that proudly profit from collegiate athletics, but see no shame in—and accept no blame for—the low graduation rates for these young people. We are frustrated with parents who, out of ignorance or greed, view recruiters as saviors, people who will save their sons from lives on the streets, people who surely have something better to offer.

Having experienced the pitfalls that await college student-athletes, we decided to do for others what was not initially done for us: heighten awareness. It is only through awareness—of self, history, and culture, among other things—that change will occur. African-American student-athletes will find it very difficult to steer themselves toward a new path without knowing how and why they reached their present destination. We offer this book to our young brothers everywhere as a compass: a reference point for their current location, and a catalyst for a much-needed change in direction.

Opportunity Awareness

The Little Rock Nine

- Ernest Green
- Thelma Mothershed
- Melba Pattillo
- Carlotta Walls
- Jefferson Thomas
- Elizabeth Eckford
- Terrance Roberts
- Gloria Ray
- Minniejean Brown

From the moment the U. S. Supreme Court handed down its landmark decision in *Brown vs. the Board of Education*, school administrators, particularly those in the South, plotted against the eventual arrival of African-American students at all-white schools. That was especially true in Little Rock, Arkansas. On September 4, 1957, three years after the Supreme Court decision, Arkansas Governor Orval Faubus ordered the National Guard to prevent nine African-American students from enrolling in all-white, Central High School.

When the students arrived at Central High, they were turned away by the National Guard and pelted with rocks, bottles, and debris as they retreated to their bus. These attacks occurred daily and were actually encouraged and perpetuated by the National Guard, whose stated mission (as announced by Faubus) was to protect the white students from the Negro students.

In his book, *It Has Happened Here*, Virgil T. Blossom, then superintendent of Little Rock

> Wake up my people, for the time is later than you think.
>
> —W. E. B. DuBois

schools, recounted the atmosphere prior to and after the students' arrival on campus. The drama was repeated daily during the early days of the confrontation:

"Here they come!" a white man near the corner yelled. He and several companions ran toward the Negroes. The boy ran away, but the Negro man did not run. He was knocked to the street and a white man kicked him in the face as the photographer watched.

At the same time, several Negro newspaper-men appeared near the school and the mob surged around them. There were no police near.

"Go home you—nigger!" somebody shouted. The reporters turned to leave, but as they did so a white man shoved one of them and a moment later the Negroes were being pummeled and kicked. Two men dragged one of them into some high grass, kicked him and slugged him and smashed the camera he was carrying . . .

Then the mob's attention was attracted away from them as a yell went up from in front of the school building: "Everybody here! The niggers are already inside . . . . Let's go get 'em!" . . . .

"Let's go in!" the mob ran around the building and surged against the police lines. A woman screamed: "I want my child out of there!" Slowly, the police fell back to the sidewalk in front of the school, but there they began using their clubs.

"Let's go home and get our shotguns," another man suggested.

"I hope," one woman shouted, "they drag out . . . dead niggers!"

In the coming days, the harassment of the Negro students intensified, with several white boys and girls identified as leaders in most of the incidents. On one occasion, a white boy blocked the sidewalk against Negro students entering the school, but they merely walked around him as

Every stabbing, gunshot wound, and death suffered throughout the history of African-American struggles in general, and the Civil Rights movement in particular, paved the way to give people like you a chance.

—Andre & Vince

Guardsmen hurried up to prevent trouble. Again, several boys walked past a Negro girl and a pile of books she carried flew up into the air. Negro students were pushed or kicked in the halls and two Negro boys were chased up a stairway before Guardsmen intervened.[1]

Nearly a month later, President Dwight Eisenhower finally intervened and sent federal troops to protect the Little Rock Nine.

That year, Daisy Bates was the president of the Little Rock chapter of the NAACP and spiritual mother to the Little Rock Nine. In the book *Children of the Dream*, Mrs. Bates is quoted as saying, "The school board selected those they felt wouldn't fight back, if opposition to their integrating were to become violent. One of the children had a heart condition." And each of them volunteered, knowing the danger in which daring to integrate with whites would place them. "There was always the possibility that someone could be killed," Mrs. Bates recalls.[2]

Despite the hostility and humiliation these courageous students endured, all members of the Little Rock Nine have become successful in their own right. All nine of these youngsters recognized their mission: be successful in integrating schools so that others would later have the opportunity. *More important, they paved a road to success, a path which all of us now have the right to travel.*

In case you did not know...

Throughout history, our people have endured endless struggles in an attempt to gain basic human rights. We have suffered the brutality of attack dogs ripping away flesh, their sharp teeth shredding men's groins, their razorlike claws slicing through women's breasts. Our people have been subjected to the horrific force of tons of water spewing from fire hoses, sometimes propelling victims through plate-glass windows. We know the terror of lynchings, the unforgettable image of those who have died from it, their heads hanging limp to one side, eyes glassy and bulging, bodies swaying in the breeze.

From Emmett Till and Medgar Evers, to Malcolm X and Dr. Martin Luther King, Jr., individuals have had their lives stolen in the struggle to liberate the minds and bodies of African-Americans. This death and suffering was the direct result of individuals who opposed a vision of equality for all people. It is the same vision that now gives you the rights your predecessors were once denied. While we could talk forever about these rights, the one we want to stress is *the right to an education equal to what other people receive.*

What we want to know is: are you taking full advantage of everything that that right offers? If you learn nothing else from this chapter, you should come to realize that the efforts of civil rights pioneers now enable you to attend institutions other than Historically Black Colleges and Universities (HBCUs). Not taking full advantage of this opportunity is a gross injustice to both yourself and your race! Why? For starters, you owe it to the thousands of people who were assaulted, humiliated, and slaughtered in the quest to ensure basic rights for African-Americans.

Second, we are in danger of extinction. African-American men are three times more likely than whites to die from AIDS. Our homicide rate is seven times higher than white men. African-American men also represent forty-five percent of the prison population. An African-American man in Harlem is less likely to reach age 65 than a resident of Bangladesh. Fifty-eight percent of African-American households are headed by women.[3] Without well-rounded, intelligent men to lead our race, African-Americans face almost insurmountable odds. Your generation is the pool from which that leadership must come, but you will have a better chance of leading our people if you have an education. The future of *all* African-Americans hinges on your being literate, skilled, and a catalyst for change.

Why you are so special

Each year, thousands of African-American students athletes are recruited by major universities. At almost the same rate, many return to their communities without a degree or even a marketable skill. In other words, they fail to take advantage of the opportunity for an education.

The graduation rate for African-American student-athletes is less than forty percent. Not everyone in this small group is adequately educated. In fact, most aren't. That's the major difference between merely getting a degree and obtaining a true education.

Young brothers make up about seventy percent of Division I basketball players and sixty percent of football players, and we are the ones least likely to graduate. For some reason, women and white athletes are taking advantage of their opportunities and we are not. And we have to stop blaming others for our failures (although the institutions recruiting us do share some of the blame).Yes, some of us come from culturally disadvantaged households, but we don't have time to cry about it. While we are bitching, others are passing us by or getting further ahead.

Opportunity Knocks

The first step to overall heightened awareness is a full understanding of the realities you face as a person of color. As American history has dictated, the opportunities for people of color have been limited. From the denial of an education to the opposition of integrated public facilities, it ain't been easy. Therefore, it is your responsibility to exploit the opportunities that are presented to you. The objective of this book is to heighten your awareness in what we feel are areas to help you do just that.

The avenues to success in academia and your career are becoming fewer and narrower. You can blame, among other things, the threatened repeal of affirmative action, corporate downsizing, and foreign competition. The point is that you should take full advantage of the diminishing opportunities life has to offer. By now, you might be tired of reading this comment, especially if you are already aware that you must make the most of your opportunities. Still, it's worth repeating because we have seen far too many African-American student-athletes (many of whom have been our friends) wasting opportunities.

As an African-American, you should aggressively work to develop ideals and institutions as opposed to programs and projects. Institutions, like solar powered machines, are independent and self-sustaining. Institutions have a vision and goals which are written into by-laws and carried out in everyday functions. Programs, on the other hand, are not self-sustaining, and require the approval of someone else for ideology and funding. They are not independent, and can be removed with the stroke of the budget ax. For us, the only way to maintain our hard-fought freedom, rights, and opportunities is through institutions. Among the first steps toward developing an institution are creating and accessing opportunities, as well as building upon them. Some young brothers and sisters in L.A. have done just that as the story in the sidebar indicates.

Realities vs. Illusions: Those Who Have Come Before You

Of the thousands of African Americans who have participated in college athletics, only a small percentage succeeded in earning a living in the sports industry (i.e., NFL, NBA, MLB). Of the remaining lot—the other ninety-nine percent that didn't make it—a small percentage completed their education and later succeeded in professional positions such as business, science, politics, etc. However, the majority of this remaining group never found success, economic viability, or positions in the professional world. Many ended up working jobs that command no more than minimum wage!

Food From the 'Hood

Shortly after the Los Angeles riots in 1992, forty students at Crenshaw High School and their biology teacher decided to reclaim the weedy, quarter-acre plot long abandoned behind the school's football field. The students simply wanted to create a community garden that would bring life back to the neighborhood and give them some hands-on science experience. They planted flowers, herbs, lettuce, collards, and other vegetables. Eventually, the kids donated some of the produce to needy South Central families and sold the rest at farmers' markets. They called their project *Food From the 'Hood.*

The Crenshaw students soon diversified. Since they had the herbs and the lettuce, they decided to create their own salad dressing called *Straight Out the Garden.* Local business leaders helped with the marketing and manufacturing, and now the dressing is sold in more than twenty-three states. Now, the student farmers are owners who expect to earn $50,000 in profits in 1995. They'll use the money to help fund scholarships.

The students run all aspects of the business, from weeding and harvesting to public relations and computer logs. *Food From the 'Hood* members have even set up a mentor system and an SAT prep program.

—**Source:** *Newsweek,* May 29, 1995

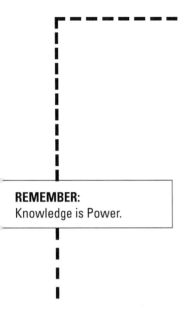

REMEMBER:
Knowledge is Power.

In analyzing why the graduation and success rates among student-athletes are so low, we find that the answer, in part, lies in students' unrealistic expectations. This is a direct result of students not being presented statistics in the area of career choices. *Such statistics would indicate that a young African-American male has a better chance of being a brain surgeon than a professional football player.* Now, we are not trying to discourage you from achieving your dreams of playing in a league. All we want is to present the facts so that you will know what you are up against. Our point is that there is more to making it in a league than just skill. One of the biggest obstacles you will face is the fact that there are not enough professional positions available for all who want to play. That means, unfortunately, that a lot of people won't make it. As cold as that statement might sound, that is the kind of knowledge that will help you prepare for the athletic and academic challenges that lie ahead.

If anyone ever told you it was uncool to be a good student and a good athlete, that person lied. It is perfectly OK to be both. It may be difficult, but it is doable. Don't believe us? Just look at Juwan Howard, Robert Smith, and Grant Hill.

Use It, Don't Lose It

We hope you now realize how crucial it is to capitalize on all opportunities. Failure to do so guarantees that the rights African-Americans suffered so valiantly for and died to attain will surely be taken away. Hopefully, as we share our experiences and those of others, we can help you avoid many of the pitfalls which have for so long prevented many of us from earning our degrees and capitalizing on all that college life has to offer. It is perfectly OK to have aspirations of life as a professional athlete, but recognize that it can be equally as rewarding to have a life not centered on sports, one in which you are happy with yourself and your family. Besides, even if you make it to a league, odds are that you will still be a young man when you retire. At that point, you will have to begin a life that may not be centered on the playing field.

PROBABILITY OF MAKING
A COLLEGE AND PROFESSIONAL TEAM IN
MEN'S BASKETBALL OR FOOTBALL

College Basketball
4,000 freshman positions each year
vs. 148,000 high school seniors

Professional Basketball
64 NBA roster positions
vs. 2,600 college seniors

Fact: 1.35 percent of high school seniors will earn scholarships to play college basketball.

Bottom line: 2.5 percent of these will make it for at least one year in the NBA.

College Football
17,500 freshman positions each year
vs. 263,000 high school seniors

Professional Football
215 NFL annual rookie roster openings vs. 9,500 college seniors

---

Fact: 3.3 percent of high school senior football players will go on to play college football

Bottom line: 2 percent of these will win jobs for at least one year in the NFL

—**Source:** 1992, *The National Federation of State High School Associations*

notes:

CHAPTER 2. DECISIONS, DECISIONS...

Do You Really Know The School For You?

You've heard it all before, this business about getting ready to embark on a wonderful journey filled with lots of opportunities. For some reason, that's how many people look at college. Sounds like a lot of hype, right? Believe it or not, preparing to enter college *is* the beginning of a journey. Along the way, you'll experience highs and lows, make decisions, and face opportunities that can have a profound effect on your entire life. The trick is to make sure that the school you pick now will offer you the best shot at achieving your dreams.

While you're trying to reach a decision, all types of folks are probably sending you mail, knocking on your door, and pulling you out of your high school classes in order to pitch their schools. Meanwhile, many of you probably already have preconceived notions about certain schools, from their winning traditions in sports to their party atmosphere. This information may have come from discussions with former high school teammates and friends, from watching bowl games, or from watching the Final Four. Regardless of how you acquired your views, this chapter is designed to help you sort out the facts so that you can make the best decision.

The first order of business is getting in the proper frame of mind. Forget that you may have been a high school superstar; discount the hype surrounding being recruited; ignore any over-zealous alumnus trying to slip you cash. In other words, clear your mind so you can make a decision that will suit you not just for the next four or five years, but the rest of your life.

> Education is our passport to the future, for tomorrow belongs to the people who prepare for it today.
>
> —Malcolm X

Since choosing a school is such a personal task, we'll skip the one-size-fits-all checklists that are included in many college guidebooks. Instead, here's what we advise you, the student-athlete, to consider before signing your life over to Walla Walla State:

Selection Criteria

1. Graduation Rates. What is the school's track record for graduating African-American student-athletes? We emphasize African-Americans because of the marked disparity between black and white student-athletes' graduation rates. According to the *1994 NCAA Division I Graduation-Rates Report*, thirty-nine percent of eligible African-American student-athletes graduated, compared with sixty percent of white student-athletes. In fact, a number of schools failed to graduate *any* African-American student-athletes. Not only that, but the report also revealed that some historically Black schools are not doing any better than some predominantly white institutions in terms of graduating their student-athletes.

2. Tradition. Do you want to be in a sports program that is always top ranked and deep at every position, or one which is up-and-coming and offers you the chance to be the missing link? We personally chose colleges with winning traditions over those with potential because both of our high schools' win-loss records sucked and we were tired of losing!

3. Academic Attitude. How do the coaching staff, academic advisers, faculty, and students view the role of the student-athlete on campus? Are you on campus *primarily* to help win games and *possibly* get an education? Is it a school of strong academic tradition, where all are expected to excel? Your personal goals should determine which one is right for you. Remember that the dual role of college athlete and college student is not an easy one. Trying to be successful at both is even tougher when those in power place too much emphasis on one or the other.

4. Academic Assistance. How much academic assistance is offered at the schools you are considering? Let's face facts: some of you brothers attend inner city high schools with less than stellar academic traditions, compared to the suburban schools that many of your future teammates and classmates have attended. The amount of academic assistance you receive and your personal desire to succeed academically will be instrumental in bridging this gap.

5. Financial Assistance. What type of financial aid is available? There is a wide range of options including full scholarships, partial scholarships, and financial aid packages. Oftentimes a financial aid package which includes grants and loans can offer more aid than a full scholarship, so don't be discouraged if you don't receive a full scholarship. The type you receive will depend on you and the institution you choose. (See Chapter 9, Money Matters, for further discussion of this topic.)

6. Racial Predominance. Can you handle being one of a handful of brothers or sisters in a class of 500 students at a historically white institution? Or, would your feel more comfortable at one of the Historically Black Colleges and Universities? One thing is certain: there is a definite difference in the social and learning atmosphere of these institutions.

7. Location. How far from home do you want to be? Maybe you live in Oregon and are thinking about a school in Florida. You love your family, the dog, and your girl, none of whom have the funds to visit you in Florida. Do not even think about asking an alum to contribute to a family travel fund; it is totally against NCAA regulations. Now, is Florida really the place for you? On the other hand, if you don't have a girl and your family gets on your nerves, maybe Florida is just the place for you.

8. Curriculum. Is there a school recruiting you that has a highly regarded program in your desired field of study? Say you have always wanted to be an engineer—not the Southern Pacific type, but the calculus working, number-crunching type that designs highways, byways, and huge electrical projects. One of the schools recruiting you may have a program in line with your aspirations.

9. Weather. The elements can have a profound effect on one's studies, athletic performance, and overall attitude. Does the thought of cold/wet/humid weather send you into a deep funk? You make the call as to what type of climate suits you.

10. Size. Is bigger better? If you are from a place like Lompac, California, and are accustomed to a high school with only 300 students, a university like Penn State, with its 37,000-plus students, might seem a tad large. On the other hand, if your high school has 3,000 students, Penn State might be just right for you, or at least close. Regardless of what you choose, remember that the number of students per class can determine the amount of individual attention you receive from professors.

Size refers not only to a college's campus, but its courses. You might assume that large universities offer more courses. The fact is that some smaller colleges can rival the largest universities in the number and variety of courses offered.

Fact Finding

Now that you have given considerable thought to what you want out of a school, it's time to identify those schools which best meet your needs. It's a tough job, but persistence and scrutiny will help determine which schools fit your profile.

Bookstores, libraries, and the colleges provide a plethora of material about colleges. In addition, there are numerous guides and booklets which describe and evaluate various schools across the country. Most schools also have promotional material such as catalogs, course listings, and videotapes that are yours for the asking.

All of these things can be good sources for achieving an overall view of the academic, traditional, and demographic aspects of a school, but we know you're interested in much more. You are probably more concerned with the intangible characteristics of a school, the things that are unique to your being an African-American. In order to better understand these characteristics, you should look to some of the following people and places for help:

- *Local NAACP chapter*
- *Black chamber of commerce*
- *Black student union and other campus groups*
- *Black fraternities and sororities*
- *Minority faculty and staff*
- *Local section of the city's daily newspaper(s)*
- *National periodicals and bookstores geared toward minorities*

Much of this fact-finding can be accomplished by telephone. If access to a phone is a problem, your high school coach may even let you use the one in his office, but be sure to get his permission first.

Narrow Your List of Schools

Take out the list of schools recruiting you and cross out the ones that don't fit your profile of desirable places. Now narrow this list to the number of schools that you can visit with respect to NCAA regulations. Remember that you are also allowed a number of unofficial visits. You are now ready to further your fact-finding mission while on your campus visits. Be advised that the coaches and their staffs will give you the most sugarcoated take on their program and will probably try to steer you from controversial subjects, people, and places. However, do not let this ploy deter you from identifying the best school for you.

By this time, you should have a pretty good understanding of the dynamics involved in choosing a school. The only thing left is to do it. Good luck, and remember that the decision will ultimately be yours.

Note to the walk-on: Although you may not have been recruited, that's no excuse for being slack in choosing a school. Realize, too, that you might be better off than someone who has only a few schools recruiting him. Unlike you, that person's options are limited. If none of the offers fit his educational and athletic criteria, he may have to accept whatever is available. You, on the other hand, have the option of playing at any school, as long as you have the right academic track record. You may even be fortunate enough to walk on and earn a scholarship. (Remember, though, that financial aid packages often exceed full scholarships.) So keep your chin up.

While on your trip, remember the following Do's and Don'ts:

DON'T: Allow others to dictate were you go, who you see, and what interests you.

DO: Look beyond the superficial frills during your trip and concentrate on the facts you discover.

DON'T: Be afraid to ask the hard questions of anyone you come in contact with.

DO: Meet as many players as possible to gauge their overall satisfaction with the program. Also, the players are an excellent way to get to the truth.

DON'T: Drink to the point that your judgment is impaired. (See *Chapter 12,* Almost Addicted)

DO: Remember that your decision can have a lasting impact on the rest of your life.

notes:

CHAPTER 3. PREGAME WARM-UPS

Before You Place Your Big Feet On Campus

So you're serious about making this trip to college? If so, the first thing we want you to determine is whether you are prepared to take this step. Of course, it's never too late to get your life on the right course, but it helps to do it as early as possible. Even you young brothers in junior high ought to be scoping your future. In other words, as soon as you get the notion that college is for you, start preparing mentally and academically. That means you should start taking school seriously, find out what it takes to be admitted into college, and learn as much about the college experience as possible.

Here are the kinds of questions you should be asking and the answers you need to know:

How can I increase my chances of getting a scholarship?

Excel in academics and athletics. First, you need to maintain a good grade point average *(GPA)* and complete the required course work. Without the GPA and the course work, you probably won't be eligible to participate in athletics. Not playing means not being seen by recruiters and, of course, missing out on athletic scholarships. Plus, your ineligibility will probably piss off your coaches and teammates who are counting on you to be part of the team. Unfortunately, as we travel around the country, we hear the same old story from high school athletes.

> For man to know himself, is for him to feel that he has no human master. For him nature is his servant; and whatsoever he wills in nature, that shall be his reward.
>
> —Marcus Garvey

So Much for the Season

Most of the guys have been working out during the summer, people are yoked and ready to kick ass this season. The season starts, and the team is living up to its expectation. You win your first league game by a tremendous margin and are looking forward to being league champions. It's Thursday, the day before your second league game, and report cards are coming out. At practice that afternoon, your coach informs you that the following guys are ineligible to play in the next game: Ray-Ray Williams, the quarterback; Philip Rodgers, your best defensive player; Peter Scarlucci, the only white guy on the team; and the list goes on. Before you know it, you have your best receiver playing quarterback and former defensive backs playing linebacker. You had thirty-eight teammates; now you have only eighteen.

Jump ahead to Friday afternoon. The game is over. You just lost 34 to 7. Hopes for a championship season just went down the drain.

—K. E. E., Class of '93

Sound familiar? If you, too, have been ineligible to play because of poor grades, don't despair, but do recognize that it takes hard work to avoid repeating this scenario. As mentioned earlier, *GPA* is extremely important and we will discuss how to better yours in Chapters 4 and 5. Taking the appropriate classes, which we address in this chapter, is also important.

To better your chances of obtaining a scholarship, you need to know all of the relevant issues, then devise and implement a strategy for achieving your goals. One of your first steps should be to determine the admissions requirements for the schools you are interested in attending.

Personal Responsibilities and Academics

What good is a stellar GPA if none of your classes count toward college requirements or, worse yet, graduation?

Finding out what classes are required to get into college and taking those classes is your responsibility. Although your school probably has people on the payroll to help, do not assume that these people will always have your best interest at heart. In fact, do not be surprised if some of the people who are supposedly being paid to help you actually resent you. They may even be a tad bit jealous of your success. That means you may not get the help you deserve from these people. That's why it is extremely important that you know what is required.

The next story shows just how important personal responsibility is for the student-athlete:

Plan B

It was my senior year and I had already accepted a scholarship to a major university, but wasn't formally accepted into the school. A few months later, I received a letter from the admissions office at the university stating that I would be denied admission due to the fact that I had not taken a lab science in high school. I thought, fine no problem, I was currently enrolled in a chemistry class and everyone knows chemistry is a lab science. Wrong. Not at my school, because the particular class I was enrolled in didn't do experiments of any kind. After this point was made clear to me, I asked my science teacher why we weren't conducting any experiments. He replied, "We don't do experiments because your dope-selling friends have stolen all of the equipment to cook and weigh that shit." The statement immediately caused irreconcilable tension between him, a conservative white man, and me, a somewhat militant Black man, and I was forced to drop his class. Fortunately, I was responsible enough to seek the advice of my mom, coaches, and administrators, and I was able to take another chemistry class (where the equipment wasn't alleged to have been stolen) and everything turned out ALL GOOD.

— J. K. L., Class of '88

See what we mean by taking responsibility for your own success? Ultimately, you are expected to know what is required for admission into college. One way to stay informed is to obtain information from the various athletic governing bodies. That's no easy task, though, since these agencies are constantly changing their rules. For practical purposes, we'll focus on what are perhaps the most important of these rules: the controversial National Collegiate Athletic Association (NCAA) *Proposition 48* and *Eligibility Clearinghouse.*

PROPOSITION 48

This NCAA regulation took effect in 1986 and has been revised a number of times. It establishes the minimum academic requirements for incoming freshmen to compete athletically as freshman at Division I or Division II schools. You might have heard that some consider it a racist rule that keeps minority athletes from realizing their dreams. After all, every minority athlete comes from an inferior ghetto school, right? Bullshit. Let's not even consider whether the regulation is racist, biased, sexist, or whatever; the bottom line is that it exists. You will not have time to lobby against it before you are accepted into college. Instead, strive for excellence, not mediocrity. That's how you can render this particular regulation irrelevant.

Besides, just because you meet the minimum NCAA requirements does not mean you will automatically meet the requirements of the particular school you want to attend. Be sure to find out the requirements of the particular school you want to attend and make *those* requirements your guide if they are more stringent than those of the NCAA.

ELIGIBILITY CLEARINGHOUSE

If you have hopes of enrolling as a freshman and participating in Division I or Division II athletics, you must be certified by the NCAA Initial-Eligibility Clearinghouse. This clearinghouse was created to ensure consistent interpretation of NCAA initial-eligibility requirements for all prospective student-athletes (i.e., to assure that a chemistry class at Los Angeles's Crenshaw High is similar to one at Chicago's King High).

In order to be certified, it is *your responsibility* to obtain and fill out the eligibility brochure and forms. You can get the forms from your high school or by contacting the NCAA directly. You may even start the process as early as your junior year in high school. To contact the NCAA directly, write to:

NCAA Clearinghouse
P.O. Box 4044
Iowa City, IA 52243-4044
Fax: (319) 337-1556

Major College Athletic Associations

Three athletic associations currently govern the majority of major college athletics. The names, addresses, and phone numbers for each are listed below. You should contact those which are relevant to your particular situation. These associations' rules may not seem fair, but they are binding in most cases. Therefore, you should be fully aware of the rules which directly affect you; they could determine whether you play or not.

1. *National Collegiate Athletic Association (NCAA)*
   6201 College Boulevard
   Overland Park, KS 66211
   (913) 339-1906

The NCAA is a private association consisting of over 500 member institutions. It has created numerous rules used to govern the athletic programs of its member institutions. The rules vary by division. Remember, you may be accepted into an NCAA member school without meeting these requirements, but do not expect to compete as a freshman.

2. *National Association of Intercollegiate*
   Athletics (NAIA)
   Kansas City, MO 64105
   (816) 842-5050

The NAIA is also a private association consisting of over 400 members. It too has created numerous regulations which are used to govern the athletic programs of member institutions.

3. *National Junior College Athletic*
   Association (NJCAA)
   P.O. Box 7305
   Colorado Springs, CO 80933
   (719) 590-9788

The NJCAA is a private association consisting of over 500 two-year institutions. It has established numerous regulations to govern its members. Member institutions are located in every state *except* California, which has its own governing body. The governing body for California is:

   California Association of Community
   Colleges (CACC)
   2017 O St.
   Sacramento, CA 95814
   (916) 444-8641

Let's Talk Standardized Tests

You are probably familiar, at least in name, with the SAT and the ACT. If you are not, and have hopes of becoming a college student-athlete, you had better familiarize yourself quickly. These examinations are administered to high school students and are used by colleges, in conjunction with core courses and GPA, to determine whether a student should be admitted.

Suppose you are an average student in high school with a GPA lower than that of a student from a school with lower grading standards. These standardized tests are meant to allow you and other students to be tested under similar conditions using the same grading standards. To many, this concept for testing favors middle class white students. Whether biased or not, these tests remain one of the primary means for determining college admission. So get over it and begin preparing to do your best. Do not use the fairness of the exam as an excuse to do poorly, because when you think about it, no one really cares about your excuses.

Below are steps you should take to prepare for these exams:

- Learn which test is required for the college you hope to attend. To find out, contact the undergraduate admissions office of the school you wish to attend. Although the SAT is still the most widely used exam, many colleges and universities (particularly those in the Midwest) are beginning to accept ACT scores as well.

- After determining which exam you need to take, familiarize yourself with that test and get with your parents, guidance counselors, or friends to develop a strategy for maximizing your score.

Bookstores and the local library should have books on preparing for these exams. Take the exam, which can be taken as many times as needed, early in your junior year so that you can retake it if your score is low. Most schools will only use your highest score.

- Enroll in courses that will give you instructions on how to take these exams. Whether you will receive benefits from an expensive test preparation course is debatable, but studies have shown that test scores can be increased, particularly in math. The benefits also depend on the quality of the course and how dedicated you are in preparing yourself.

- Since these exams are, in part, geared to determine what you have already learned, it's obvious that you should learn as much as possible in the classroom. If you come from one of those high schools where it is almost impossible to learn in the classroom, or you just thought it was uncool to do so, put this book down and start studying. You are going to look real faulty when some of your boys get scholarships and you do not.

Testing, testing. . .

Vince has taken test prep courses on two occasions, once when preparing for the Certified Public Accountant (CPA) exam, which we are proud to say he passed on his first try. The other was the Graduate Management Admissions Test (GMAT). Vince had this to say: "The review course for the CPA was good. The main thing it did for me was to identify the relevant concepts that would be on the exam. In contrast, the review course I took in order to prepare for the GMAT was terrible. In fact, the first time I took the exam I didn't bother to turn my booklet in." The GMAT is similar to the SAT or ACT, except that it is for graduate business schools. So we urge you to carefully consider all the options when deciding whether to take a review course.

TIPS FOR MAXIMIZING YOUR SCORE

1. Prepare in order to score as high as possible, not just to obtain the minimum requirements established for admission.

2. Be disciplined in your preparation by establishing a routine which you follow every day.

3. Prepare flash cards to memorize key concepts, facts, and ideas. This stored knowledge will give you added confidence on test day, as well as speed up problem solving, particularly in math.

4. Take as many practice tests as humanly possible. This repetition will not only familiarize you with the type of questions on the exam, but will also increase your test taking speed, since these are timed exams. (Be sure to use actual prior exams.)

5. Be sure to take all practice tests under actual test-taking conditions (i.e., time yourself, turn off the phone, etc.)

6. Starting today, begin to read as much outside material as possible. Reading will increase your comprehension, vocabulary, and verbal reasoning. Besides, it's actually fun.

7. Finally, you should chill out the day before the exam. Intense studying at this point will create more problems (i.e., being stressed out). Keep things in the proper perspective by remembering that even though your future may rest, in part, on your score, it is still only one test of many that you will take in your life time.

Marketing Your
Number One Asset: You

Everyone in your school knows what a great student-athlete you are. Everyone from opposing coaches, players, and cheerleaders fear your sweet jumper, but do the right people know who you are? If you are from a school or league which traditionally does not get much ink (let alone TV air time), then you and your coaches may have to do some additional marketing. You may have to market yourself to become a member of that nationally ranked team you have been dreaming of since the sixth grade. Numerous professional athletes have mastered the concept of self-promotion: Dennis Rodman, Brian Bosworth, and Deion Sanders, to name a few. Here's an overview of possible marketing techniques:

1. Start your marketing plan as soon as you begin to show a little dominance in your sport. This will help give you name recognition among the community, reporters, and opposing coaches. These people will vote on post-season honors that you hope to win.

2. Get your coach or some other person in authority to contact the local newspaper after each game (as soon as you walk off the field, because reporters do not like printing old news) to give them your stats. Again, this adds to your name recognition.

3. At the start of your sophomore or junior year, you or your coach should draft letters to the head coaches of schools you are interested in attending. These letters should resemble a cover letter for a job interview. The letters should say what a wonderful person you are

and tell of all the other activities you participate in while still maintaining a solid GPA. Include a page similar to a resume which highlights all of your athletic accomplishments (i.e., awards, strength, speed, stats).

4. Make sure that someone videotapes as many of your games as possible, even if this means you have to save money and buy a video camera for someone else to use for taping you.

SAMPLE LETTER

Kelvin Johnson
8152 Seminary Street
Detroit, MI 48201
May 15, 19XX

Mr. John Chaney.
Head Basketball Coach
Temple University
Philadelphia, PA 19120

Dear Coach:

I am in my junior year at Cass Tech. High School, where I am a 6'3" starting point guard on an up-and-coming team which continues to improve each year. As a freshman, I lead the team in assists averaging 8.3 per game. I also averaged 12 points and 5 rebounds per game. In my sophomore year I averaged 10.7 assists, 15 points, and 7 rebounds per game, which earned second team All-League honors. This past season, I led the league in assists at 11.8 per game, was second in scoring averaging 19.7 per game, and was named to the All-League team and second team All State. Next year, I hope to be an instrumental in helping my team compete for the championship.

I am very interested in attending Temple University upon my graduation. I believe that my athletic and scholastic accomplishments make me uniquely qualified to be a valuable addition to your program. I would appreciate it if you would consider me as a possible scholarship candidate.

Please find enclosed a brief resume of my athletic and academic accomplishments along with several newspaper articles. In addition, I have provided a list of coaches and reporters who can vouch for my ability and character.

Thank you in advance for your time and consideration.

Sincerely,

Kelvin Johnson

5. Have your coach nominate you for any and every award, honor, or trophy available. You may not win, but it will increase your name recognition. Hype can sometimes create opportunity for you, then you have to back it up.

6. Have your coach or another person contact the high school sports reporter for the local paper. Come up with a human interest story surrounding your team and try to get a reporter to write about it. Reporters often look for good stories to follow up on. (See Chapter 13, You and Scoop.)

7. Tell everyone who will listen that you're a damn good player, and where you would like to attend college. Someone may hear you who has "pull" at one of the schools and put a word in for you. (This is a part of networking, which we discuss at length in Chapter 10.)

SAMPLE RESUME

PERSONAL

Kelvin Johnson
8152 Seminary Street
Detroit, MI 48201

(313) 892-0000

Coach John Doe
Cass Technical High School
1564 Second Avenue
Detroit, MI 48203

(313) 872-0000

Height: 6'3"   Weight: 185   Vertical: 48"   Wingspan: 120"

ACADEMICS:

G.P.A.:   2.87/4.0
SAT: Math-580   Verbal-460
College Prep. courses including the required NCAA core courses. Inroads Program Participant

ATHLETICS: (per game)

	Assists	Points	Rebounds
Freshman:	8.3	12.1	5.3
Sophomore:	10.7	15.3	7.0
Junior:	11.8	19.7	8.2

First Team All-League, Second Team All-State, Team MVP as a junior, All-League Football

8. Try to identify recruiters who will be in the area to look at other players, or who will be attending one of your games to see your opponent. Have your coach contact them and put your name in their ear. This may help you get a longer look.

9. One of the most important things to remember is: handle your business and stay out of trouble. Colleges do not typically like people who are constantly prone to trouble. These words of advice will also be relevant if you are fortunate enough to continue your career into the professional ranks. At that point, not handling your personal business may cost you thousands of dollars (i.e., endorsement, fines, etc.)

You've Signed The Letter of Intent, Now What?

Before signing the National Letter of Intent (NLI):

1. Make sure you thoroughly understand the NLI and all of its provisions.

2. Involve others (i.e., parents, coaches, mentors, principal, counselor) who can help decipher the provisions.

3. Make sure you have thoroughly explored your options before signing early. CCA has designated times for signing the NLI, depending upon your sport. However, some sports allow you to sign early.

4. Determine under what conditions your scholarship and/or aid can be revoked.

5. Ask recruiters about the stability of the program (i.e., coaching changes, NCAA investigations).

Additional Resources:

Athletic Scholarships
Facts on File Inc.
460 Park Ave. South
New York, NY 10016

Athletic Scholarships: A Compete Guide
Conway Greene Publishing Co.
11000 Cedar Ave
Cleveland, OH 44106

Free Money for Athletic Scholarships
Henry Holt and Company, Inc.
115 W. 18th St.
New York, NY 10011

We have already tried to introduce you to one of the key concepts of this guide and that concept is **STUDENT-ATHLETE**. As you prepare for college, you need to prepare for each of these roles. First, we'll discuss more advanced academic preparation than we have previously in

On the Dotted Line

Hold up: Let's talk about the National Letter of Intent (NLI). You may not be aware of the true nature of this contract, which can adversely affect your athletic future.

The NLI is an official document administered by the Collegiate Commissioners Association (CCA). Once signed, it obligates you to compete athletically at the school you have selected. After you sign, all other schools who abide by the rules of the NLI agree not to recruit you any further.

You are the only one with something to lose from signing the NLI. (In fact there is no law which says you have to sign it.) There have been some cases where blue chip athletes have not signed NLIs, and were still offered scholarships. However, the NLI is the current standard, and most schools will probably not offer you aid without your signing it. As mentioned, once it is signed you are obligated to that particular school. If you do not uphold this obligation and decide to enroll in another school which abides by the NLI, *you can not participate in athletics for a full two years.*

On the flip side, the coaches recruiting you have no obligation to remain at the institution once you decide to attend. For example, say you are being recruited by UCLA on a track scholarship. You accept the scholarship and sign the NLI because you want to be coached by Bob Kersee. However, after signing, you learn that Kersee has decided to take a position at TCU. Unfortunately, you are stuck at UCLA, unless you sit out for two years. Kersee can leave without penalty and immediately continue his coaching career. This example illustrates one of the inconsistencies associated with signing the NLI.

this chapter. Next, we'll discuss more ways to prepare athletically. Which side of the phrase you want to put the most emphasis on is up to you. We only hope that you remember which side lasts the longest.

Advanced Preparation

PART 1: ADVANCED ACADEMIC PREPARATION

Here, we are referring to the advance preparation of a successful college student—one who ultimately graduates in the field of his choice, not that of the athletic department's guidance counselors. We don't want to be accused of knocking guidance counselors hired by the athletic departments. Most will probably have your best interest at heart, but due to forces beyond their control, they may not always be able to guide you in the direction that best benefits you. This phenomenon can best be explained by understanding the dynamics surrounding major college sports programs: Coaches are hired to win games and their success and admiration comes from winning. This can put pressure on all those working for the program to create an environment which is conducive to winning games. A winning environment does not necessarily coincide with your best academic interests. Thus, guidance counselors can sometimes be pressured into guiding you in a direction which best benefits the team. You probably can not blame them. They have bills to pay just like the rest of us. But you should be aware of the environment in which they work.

PART 2: ADVANCED ATHLETIC PREPARATION

Obviously, this aspect deals with athletic performance. Unfortunately, for those who will pay your tuition, this may be their main focus. Remember that once you set foot on campus, you may no longer be the superstar you once were. The action will be faster and more intense, and you will be surrounded by many other former high school standouts. But don't despair; if you weren't quali-

NOTE:
Contact the specific schools which interest you to get information on what is expected of college freshmen academically. There are also numerous books on the subject.

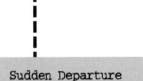

Sudden Departure

I signed my NLI with the understanding that my coach would be there for all four years. However, a year after my arrival, he was fired for violating numerous NCAA rules. I was given two options. First, to stay and not be able to go on road trips or compete in any championship meets; second to transfer and sit out for two years. I chose to stay and suffer. As a consequence of the sanctions, I feel that I was never able to reach my full potential as a world class track athlete.

—D. J., Class of 1992

fied to compete at this level, they wouldn't have wasted time recruiting you. From this point on, your only concern should be whether your athletic skills are improving. This includes everything from increasing your vertical to maintaining the right attitude (discussed in Chapter 8.) Here are a few suggestions to consider before reporting to camp:

- Sit down with your high school coaches and evaluate your strengths and weaknesses. You may have already done this when you developed your marketing plan.

- Identify specific drills and/or exercises you can use to improve on your weaknesses. Once identified, establish a routine and follow it regularly.

- Contact the coach who recruited you and/or players you met on your trip to find out what tests you will have to take at camp. Determine what skills impress coaches the most.

- Get to know the strength/conditioning coaches at colleges in your area. They have a wealth of knowledge and may be able to help you physically prepare for the challenges awaiting you.

- Get into the best shape of your life. Practice will be much more grueling than high school, and the last thing you need to worry about is "sucking wind" unnecessarily.

- Mentally prepare for whatever challenges arise. Refuse to be intimidated by anyone. You may want to use some type of visualization technique. (There are many good books on the subject of visualization.) Use them to work on your game!

Nine Things Every Incoming Freshman Should Know About

1. **Personal Hygiene**: grooming, teeth, anti-perspirant.
2. **Eating Etiquette:** conversation, meal selection, use of utensils.
3. **Cooking:** food groups, balanced diets, et cetera.
4. **Laundry:** washing, ironing, maintenance.
5. **Stress Management:** meditation, Sega, music.
6. **Effective Communication:** written, oral, body language.
7. **Computers:** word processing, spreadsheets, on-line communication.
8. **Banking:** establishing checking and savings accounts, check writing.
9. **Establishing and Maintaining Credit:** Visa/ MasterCard, utilities, loans, et cetera.

By the way, these principles will assist you not only in the transition to college life, but will also help make you a better husband, father, and overall person. Best of luck on what we hope is the start of a successful career—and don't forget to kick some ass in the process.

notes:

How Will I Fit In?

A Whole New World

Man, when I first got on campus my ass got lost. I had never seen that many heads in one place. In most of my classes, there was only a handful of brothers. Everyone else was either white or Asian. I didn't even see any Latino brothers. Then again, my classes are so big, maybe I missed somebody.

I got this one sociology class that has 450 people in it, craziest thing you ever seen. It seems like everyone in there is smart. You should hear some of the questions that the white boys be asking, crazy shit that doesn't make any sense. I used to keep my mouth shut, cause like my mama used to say, "If you ain't got nothing intelligent to say, don't say nothing at all." Then I realized that they were not that smart, they just routinely spoke the "King's English." At this point in my career, I realize that when I have to I can speak the King's English, too. In fact I am bilingual. Now they can't shut me up, because I can talk that King's English shit when and where I want to.

You know they never stressed academics around this camp, so when I got there I had to learn how to really study. It was helluva difficult at first, but I think I've finally got it figured out. I have got three classes in a row, and they are all on different sides of campus. They only give you ten minutes between each class, so you got to move. By the time I get out it's lunch time, so I head on over to the Union. It's a trip, 'cause when you walk in segregation hits you right in the face. All the Black folks over here, the Asians over there, the whites over there, etc. This is supposed to be the '90s where that shit is not mandatory, but people do it anyway. And they have so many different kinds of women on campus. Damn near all of them fine.

(continued on next page)

I remember when I was in my teens, I met all those loving white people at Manhasset. Then I went to Syracuse, ran chin first into overt racism. Someone had changed all the rules, forgotten to tell me.

—Jim Brown

Anyway, after I deal with all this everyday, it's time for the easy part: practice. I just go into the locker room and chill before we go out on the field. Nobody (outside of the coaches) can bother you down there. We're like one big family. It would be straight if classes could be like that, too. All in all, this year has been pretty tough, but I think I can handle it. Come 1998, my ass will be graduating.

—J. T., Class of '98
(Addressing former high school team mates)

As the story illustrates, adjusting to campus life can be difficult. The key is to learn the rules of the game as quickly as you can. Brother J. T. did fairly well for a rookie. Almost immediately, he grasped the concept of enhancing his vocabulary and the need at times to speak the "King's English." As you can see, he can talk one way around his boys, as well as flip the script and speak the "King's English" to others. The importance of this kind of versatility cannot be underestimated. J.T.'s story touches on a lot of what's involved in the social transition from high school to college. It also is proof of the progress you can make when your awareness level is high.

We thought we would allow Lamont McKim, doctoral candidate, to flex his linguistic muscles on the importance of being able to communicate in the "King's English."

The Importance of Linguistic Expression

For most student-athletes, like most people in general, ignorance of the importance of language as a vehicle of verbal and nonverbal expression has been and is a fertile source of false belief. This belief stems from an underdeveloped knowledge and understanding of the role that language plays in fostering, maintaining, and sustaining social cohesion. For it is through language that all creatures communicate.

For many student-athletes, the importance of being bilingually competent—maintaining one's own language while developing the linguistic competence to thrive and excel in the dominant culture—can not be emphasized enough. Because the educational systems value "standard" English and the written tradition, it is important for the student-athlete to master this mode of expression in the academic setting. Although some nontraditional students fear being ostracized by their peers for mastering the "King's English," this mastery should not be construed as a threat to the students' self- or sociocultural identity. In short, this mastery is a practical approach to, if nothing else, one's self-promotion and marketing. After all, this will be the dominant mode of expression on standardized entrance exams (SAT, ACT, GRE, LSAT, GMAT, MCAT, etc.). It will be the dominant mode of expression in classroom discussions, exams, and writing assignments in one's academic tenure, as well as outside of the classroom when college is over. For those student-athletes who go on to become superstars, it is the mode of expression that results in "big-time" endorsement contracts. And for those student-athletes who seek postcollegiate careers unrelated to sports, it is the dominant mode of expression on Wall Street, at IBM, Xerox, Proctor & Gamble, etc.

Thus, a student-athlete must be vast and flexible in his/her approach to developing the necessary communication tools. Just because someone else is not intelligent, committed, or, perhaps, courageous enough to appreciate the strength in being fluent in more than one culture doesn't mean you have to imitate their ignorance.

—Lamont M. McKim *(Doctoral Candidate)*

When it comes to being bilingual, you really have an advantage over your white counterparts. Most of them will never become fluent in what is traditionally known as "Black English," for it is an unwritten language created when our ancestors were forcibly brought to this country. The slave-masters purposely separated our ancestors from others of their tribes in order to prevent them from communicating with one another. But our people were intelligent, and quickly created new languages that included both tribal and European words. One such language developed was called Gullah Creole or Plantation Creole. Any reputable linguistist will tell you that this was and still is a legitimate language with its own well-focused grammar and syntax. It was from these languages that Black English got its start. So don't allow anyone to tell you that Black English is not a legitimate form of expression.

For many student-athletes, becoming bilingual is one of the many new things you will deal with on campus. But issues even larger than that must be addressed. In this chapter, we will describe the social differences between the college campus and the various communities that a student-athlete might come from. We will also explain why the differences between these two environments often cause difficulties for the student-athletes in these situations.

Social Circles

We will start by dividing the community into social circles. Be advised that some circles do not apply to all communities; however, the core is basic to most communities.

- **Family Circles.** This interaction covers, but is not limited to, your immediate family. Extended family, such as cousins, aunts, and uncles, also play a prominent role.

- **Academic Circles.** Includes, but is not limited to, the classroom. Many of your classmates will also overlap into your social life.

- **Daily Social Circles.** Includes the people you hang out with before, during, and after school.

- **Religious Circles.** Includes religious and spiritually based relationships (i.e., church members, ministers).

- **Neighborhood Circles.** Casual friends and enemies who live in close proximity, some of whom you see daily (i.e., neighbors, kids you grew up with, thugs, merchants).

- **Athletic Circles**. Interaction related to athletics (i.e., practice, weight training, etc.)

(See "High School to College" diagram, page 59.)

TRANSITION FROM THE INNER CITY TO THE COLLEGE CAMPUS

It does not take a genius to figure out that the inner city and the predominately white college campus are as far apart culturally, socially, and environmentally as the North and South poles are geographically. As a result, the drastic differences between your community and the college campus may leave you feeling alienated. That feeling of alienation could have a major impact on your ability to excel in college.

Studies have shown that many student-athletes such as yourself excel in areas outside of sports *while in high school.* This fact is documented in the 1987 Women's Sports Foundation Report titled: "Minorities in Sports: The Effect of Varsity Participation on the Social, Educational, and Career

Mobility of Minority Students." This report established that—in stark contrast to black nonathletes—*black high school athletes have higher self-esteem, are more active in extracurricular activities other than sports, are more involved in the community at large, aspire to be some form of community leader, and have better grade point averages and standardized test scores.*

These facts illustrate that some of the problems faced by the African-American student-athlete start after high school, during the transition into college. We have outlined seven basic problems which arise during this transitional period. These problems often result in an unsuccessful adjustment to college life, which translates into an unsuccessful academic career. This outline will give you insight as to what problems you might encounter as an African-American student-athlete in transition.

The Seven Basic Problems

1. Lack of familiar social circles on campus. The social circle with the least variation from *community* to *campus* is the one which involves *athletics*. This can be a problem because involvement in athletics could lessen your exposure to the other five circles, thus leaving you uncomfortable when you are out of your element. The academic, study, daily, religious, and party circles may all play an important role in your personal development, yet time spent in these areas will be limited because of your commitment to athletics. Therefore, you will be pressed to make sure that the relatively small amount of time you spend in these circles is put to good use. It is important for you to build relationships outside of the athletic circle, if you are to fully enjoy and benefit from the entire college experience.

Possible Solutions: After recognizing that there are differences between your old environment and the campus environment, you may recognize the difficulty in adapting. It will help for you to learn some degree of *social conformity.* Conforming means learning what behavior is acceptable and what boundaries exist on campus. Talking to successful older players, mentors, and other former student-athletes will help you understand the boundaries. Then you can learn to live and progress within them. These boundaries (i.e., rules) will dictate how much you have to adjust your behavior. Once you feel you have adjusted, practice staying in bounds. It is also imperative that you establish relationships outside of sports to further your personal development. Practice makes perfect in anything, so

Me and Chuck Dee

One night I was chillin' in my room, listening to some P.E., when this white boy from down the hall started pounding on my door. When I opened the door and asked him what his problem was, he started talkin' shit about my music being too loud. After about two minutes, I had to check his ass to let him know what time it was. He didn't know who he was messin' with, cause I ain't from around here. Back home, we don't play that shit. I've seen people die for less.

Anyway, all I remember is them pulling me off of him. Next thing you know the boyz rolled up, and took my ass to jail. I been on probation ever since, all because some punk ass wanted to play tough guy. Cold part is, it wasn't worth it. They kicked me out of the dorms, and I lost my starting job. My relationship with my coaches was never the same. All over some B.S.

—D. C., Class of '91

the more you interact with different groups of people, the more polished you will become. Draw on some of your community experiences, such as being confident, mentally tough, and fearless in difficult situations.

Something Good From The 'Hood

Everyone does not grow up in the inner city, but those of us who have often rely on some valuable traits that can work to our advantage in everyday situations:

- **Mental Toughness.** You may not be the type who is mentally intimidated or discouraged. This toughness will help you persist in pursuing your goals.

- **Physical Toughness.** You might have the ability to defend yourself against aggression, which is always a plus. This kind of toughness will make you less vulnerable to physical intimidation in hostile environments.

- **Fearless Attitude.** You might have experienced much more difficult and life-threatening situations, so less threatening problems will seem small by comparison and less intimidating. This attitude will make you less likely to press the panic button when problems arise.

- **Awareness of the Hustle.** You might have seen people get hustled, and your awareness of the games that people play is heightened. This lessens your chances of being suckered.

- **Motivation.** You might be aware of the plight of the masses of our people. This awareness should serve as a personal and economic motivation for you to succeed in your endeavors.

When applied correctly, these qualities help shape your character and common sense, and—all things being equal—give you a competitive edge.

To assist you in developing a better understanding of the difficulties in moving from one environment to another, we have included the following diagram of how the two environments match up:

HIGH SCHOOL TO COLLEGE: FROM DAY TO NIGHT

COMMUNITY	COLLEGE	VARIATIONS	POTENTIAL PROBLEMS
Family	None		Lacking parental support system
Academic	Academic	College classes larger & impersonal, few if any African-Amer. professors	May lack academic preparation & may feel intimidated/out of place. Few potential mentors
Daily Social	Daily Social	More people, different people, unfamiliar faces	Little experience interacting with white students, may lack skills to make friends outside of athletics
Religious	Religious	Pre-dominantly white conservative, no feeling of extended family	Not the spiritual bedrock you may be used to, may feel discomfort when asking for support & they may not understand your situation
Neighborhood	Daily Social	Dorm life can be lonely, neighbors often act like strangers	May feel unaccepted by peers in dorms, may lead to isolation from neighbors, and athlete might miss opportunity to socialize away from sports.
Athletic	Athletic	Fewer African American Coaches, higher expectations & pressure	Lacking mentor relationship with coach, high school coach may have have provided support outside of athletics

2. Unrealistic Expectations. The basic premise of this problem deals with lack of awareness among student-athletes (see Chapter 1). The main contributor to unrealistic expectations is the lack of opportunity awareness. Student-athletes are not aware that they have a better chance of being a brain surgeon than they do of playing a professional sport[5]. The conditioning of the African-American student-athlete begins at a young age, when the only images of success that we see are of athletes and entertainers. This may lead to more time spent on the playground than with the books.

Possible Solutions. One solution is to heighten *overall awareness.* If we can open your eyes to the realities of making it in the pros, then we have successfully laid the groundwork for attitude adjustment (i.e., student first, athlete second). This will not be an easy task. The need is for greater exposure to African-American business professionals and alternatives outside of sports. This will allow your dreams and heroes to be formulated in academic *and* athletic circles. The following facts spell out your chances of making it in professional football — and the chances of making it in other sports are just as poor:

Facts about Pro Football

Fact: *3.3 percent of high school senior football players will play college football*

Bottom Line: *2 percent of these will win jobs for at least one year in the NFL*

—*Source: 1992, The Nat. Federation of State High School Associations*

---

3. Coping with the components of racism.

Racism (hostilities, institutional bias, and discrimination) is much more complicated than having someone call you a nigger. According to Gordon W. Allport, author of *The Nature of Prejudice*, racism manifest itself in various degrees. The majority of Allport's categories are present on college campuses; all of them tarnish the college experience. Below, we will outline his categories, plus cite examples of how they have played out in the past and in some cases, continue to do so today.

Antilocution. This is a situation where people who have prejudices talk about them with like-minded friends and occasionally with strangers. Although there is no overt action, the nature of this thought pattern will lead to segregation.

On Campus: People in this category usually separate themselves from the race they dislike. You might have classmates or people in your dorm who behave in this manner. They might speak to, even briefly socialize with, you, but on the inside there is a degree of prejudice and discomfort for these people when around other races.

Avoidance. If the prejudice is more intense, it leads the individual to avoid members of the disliked group, even at the cost of considerable inconvenience to the person. This represents a more conscious effort on the individual's part to isolate himself from the disliked group.

On Campus: People in this category go *way* out of their way to avoid the disliked group. You may know a classmate who heads in the

Once Upon a Time, I Was a Star

My senior year, I lit the whole conference up. I had fourteen touchdowns in eleven games, including a three-touchdown performance against USC. I was drafted in the third round by the Seattle Seahawks. My first year, I was on IR part of the season, and by my third year I was seeing little time. The following season, I was released. I was then forced into a job I did not want because with no degree, my options were limited. *I never expected not to make it in the NFL.* It wasn't that I didn't have the ability; it was a matter of politics and dollars. Had I known then what I know now, I would have been more competitive in the classroom.

—D.G., Class of '84

opposite direction when she sees you, or even a person in the dorms who will leave the bathroom every time you come in.

Discrimination. The prejudiced person makes detrimental distinctions of an active sort. He is determined to exclude all members of the disliked group (whether they belong to a certain race, sex, or religion) from employment, housing, political rights, educational and recreational opportunities, churches, hospitals, or some other social privileges. This is one aspect of institutionalized racism.

On Campus: One example of this kind of discrimination is the small number of African-American students and faculty. The hiring practices of colleges reflects institutional bias to some degree, and account for the small percentage of African-American faculty. Biased educational policies in the public schools often leave African-American students academically unprepared for college. Clearly, institutional racism has a broad effect on the racial makeup of college campuses.

Physical Attack. Heightened emotions fueled by prejudice may lead to acts of violence or semiviolence.

On Campus: The individuals in this category are not limited to people who follow hate groups, but those who physically attack people based on their race, creed, or sex. This could occur in the basketball gym, where a player (who is anti-black) might physically attempt to abuse another player. It could also occur in the dorms, where you might encounter some violent male who aggressively promotes racial violence.

Extermination. Lynchings, massacres, and the Hitlerian program of genocide mark the ultimate degree of violent expression of prejudice.

On Campus: As little as twenty-five years ago, there were lynchings on or close to college campuses in the South; however, this type of violent expression is now rare. We still see remnants of it today in the form of police officers shooting unarmed African-Americans, murders of unarmed African-Americans (i.e., Howard Beach, Bensonhurst, LaTisha Harlins), and occasional mob behavior on the part of racist students.

All of these degrees of racism have a negative effect on the victim. As a student-athlete, you may or may not be aware of what is going on. You might even attempt to block out the effects, but you will feel them on a subconscious level. The feelings you may experience include low self-esteem, anger, isolation (more to come on isolation) frustration, rejection, and any number of other negative feelings. We are attempting to warn you of these potential situations so you can prepare to deal with them. Truth be known, there is no foolproof safeguard against these problems, but being prepared may lessen the shock.

True education has one purpose and one purpose only—to help students become aware of their own power, so they can function in their own best interest.

—Dr. John Hendrik Clark

Possible Solutions:

- *Campus Groups.* This includes the African-American student union, ad hoc student committees, coalitions, etc. Another option would be to start a support group for student-athletes. Discussions within these groups will help you vent frustrations and find emotional support.

- *Cultural Roots.* This includes immense self-study (see suggested Reading List), and developing knowledge of your culture. In doing so, you will begin to realize the significant historical contributions of your ancestors, thus raising your self-esteem and self-awareness, and making you less vulnerable to racist attitudes. Knowing your history provides you with the truth about our people, and as the saying goes, *"The truth will set you free."*

- *Watchdog Agencies.* If you encounter racism in any form, you should not take matters into your own hands unless you are forced to defend yourself. Agencies, both on and off campus, exist to help protect your civil rights. They include:
  - Campus Minority Affairs Department
  - University Office of Human Relations
  - National Urban League
  - NAACP

- *Mentor Relationships.* This includes but is not limited to professors, administrators, and counselors. These people will help guide you, as they have been down this road long before you. Their experiences can be of great value if you listen intently and follow some of their advice.

Campus I S O L A T I O N

Isolation on campus can have a negative effect on a person. Below are two categories of social isolation. Keep in mind, though, that racism is *not* the sole cause of social isolation for the college student-athlete.

Reasons for social isolation from the general student body

Racial stereotypes. Other students' invalid fears of violence and doubts about the intelligence and academic ability of African-American student-athletes.

Limited social time. No time for anything outside of school and sports. *No Extracurricular Activity.*

Lack of in-class networking. No effort on student-athletes' part to build relationships with fellow students. This may stem from feelings of isolation that are also caused by stereotyping. However, *this is no excuse not to network.*

Lack of campus involvement. No involvement in politics or policy setting on campus. May stem from student-athletes not perceiving themselves as having a relevant voice, or as lacking time to participate.

Cultural Differences. Oftentimes, people with similar cultural backgrounds prefer to hang out with one another, and choose not to be around other cultures (i.e., prefers: rock over rap, golf over hoop, etc.).

Reasons for social isolation from African American students

Lack of campus involvement. No involvement in politics or policy setting as it pertains to African-Americans on campus. Student-athletes often believe that race politics do not affect them.

Athletic stereotypes. African-American students sometimes buy into the belief that student-athletes are merely "dumb jocks." This is caused in part by African-American students repeating stereotypes they learn from society, as well as focusing on athletes who are socially withdrawn in the classroom. Often, other students equate that withdrawal with lack of intellect.

Jealousy. This attitude is caused by the misconception that all athletes are spoiled, don't have to work for anything, and that society tends to put athletes on a pedestal. Again, the general student body and media shape this perception, and it is reinforced when student-athletes return from tournaments and bowl games with nice mementos *(i.e., .pictures, rings, watches, sweat suits).*

4. Community-based support systems. In times of stress, there are few organizations on campus for you to turn to for support, outside of the Black student union, the African-American studies department, and the campus mental health group. Sometimes, you will need spiritual guidance and counseling from an Afrocentric perspective. This type of moral support exists on some campuses; however, such support is often understaffed and underfunded. Campus support groups usually will not provide you with the same love as the African-American community. This is when you may begin to miss your former community circles of family and church.

Possible Solutions: Make a conscious effort to build reciprocal relationships within the African-American community. If you are unfamiliar with the area, ask fellow students and teammates for ideas. Maybe go to church with them, or go to their old high school when they visit. You will usually be well received, and much love and support often follows. This will help you deal with losing your old community circles. You should also consider volunteer tutoring, weekend sports camps, and programs involving community youths. If no camps exist, consider starting your own. Help is almost always needed in these areas. These support groups can serve as a substitute for some of the support systems you knew in your community. Quite often, giving of yourself is the best gift of all, and it will be greatly appreciated and reciprocated.

5. Lack of self-esteem. During the transition from high school to college, the student-athlete's perception of himself is drastically altered. Dr. Richard Lapchick, of the Center for the Study of Sport in Society at Northeastern University, discusses this issue in his book, *Five Minutes to Midnight; Race and Sport in the 1990s.* He laments: "The primary question which now must be asked is, what happens to the black athlete between high school and college that seems to totally change how he perceives himself?"

As we said earlier in this chapter, the African-American student-athlete's perception and self-esteem may change because of his new environment and social circles. But there's usually more to it than that.

This negative perception can also result from the belief that college is full of supersmart people who come from supersmart high schools. For some student-athletes, this way of thinking is shaped at an early age. For inner city student-athletes, the nice suburban high schools housed in impressive facilities that they see when they play road games, coupled with media perceptions of suburbia, help perpetuate this mentality. You might see the other students as coming from academically better backgrounds, and this might sometimes be true. Unfortunately, this way of thinking sometimes can lead to intimidation in the classroom, at which point the tendency is to withdraw and not ask questions. You might perceive yourself as less intelligent than your non-African-American counterparts, which can also lead to low academic expectations. Academic preparation and how much you apply yourself gives you the grounding necessary to succeed. If someone does better than you academically, it is not necessarily true that they are more intelligent, just that they are more prepared.

Another form of misperception affects young brothers from upper to middle class families who try to act like people who live in the 'hood. This behavior is often shaped by what they see in rap videos, TV, and movies, as well as peer pressure

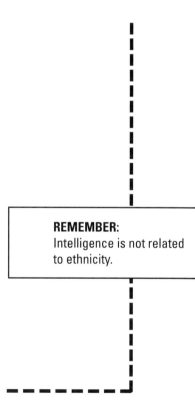

REMEMBER:
Intelligence is not related to ethnicity.

the sport of learning

from those who do come from the 'hood. Oftentimes, peers tend to look at them as being bourgeois, thus the affluent brothers try to act more like the brothers from the tough neighborhoods. These kids often feel that they are out of the mainstream of African-American behavior, or that their economic status somehow makes them "pseudo" or "soft." Sometimes, kids from the suburbs get into *more trouble* than kids from the inner city because they attempt to do more heinous things to prove how hard they can be.

Possible Solutions: Dismiss the idea that other students are in some way genetically more intelligent than you are. Intellect is relative to the amount of time you spend developing it, and the environment in which it is developed. The bottom line is that if a student comes from a socially and economically better environment, that student might be better prepared for college. That does not mean there is no hope for other students. If you are a student with academic deficiencies, then you need to get help (i.e., get your weight up). How much you apply yourself will directly impact your level of success. *The Bell Curve* is a bunch of total nonsense written by two men who refuse to accept that socioeconomic factors play a role in developing intelligence, and who also fail to recognize that a test compiled by affluent whites is not an accurate gauge of intelligence for anyone other than whites. This ridiculous theory has been around for decades, and it has been thoroughly disproved by the scientific community.

The Bell Curve Analysis:
Genetic Inferiority Among Africans

According to Charles Murray and the late Harvard psychologist Richard Herrnstein, Blacks as a group are intellectually inferior to whites, which leads them to a dead serious attack on affirmative action. Murray and Hernstein say that the evidence of a Black-white IQ gap is overwhelming. They think the difference helps explain why many Blacks seem destined to remain mired in poverty, and they insist that whites and Blacks alike must face up to the reality of black intellectual disadvantage.

Source: *Newsweek,* Oct. 24, 1994, "IQ: Is it destiny?"

Another solution is to develop a strong cultural foundation. This can be achieved by reading books on African history, language, culture, etc. (See our suggested readings.) Studying the accomplishments of your ancestors will help you realize your potential. Among other things, you will learn that Africans' contributions changed the course of history. These contributions included the Egyptian origin of geometry, philosophy, and astronomy; and the Moorish Empire that ruled Spain for 900 years and taught the Europeans (Columbus included) about navigation, sewage systems, how to use salt to preserve meat, etc. Information such as this disputes any and all claims that Africans are genetically inferior. However, if you don't educate yourself, the rhetoric from *The Bell Curve* analysis might sound believable.

6. Failure of urban schools to adequately prepare students for college. The problems of our nation's public school system in general, and urban schools in particular, have grown at an alarming rate over the last twenty years. These problems include lack of funding, inadequate facilities, lower curriculums levels, high drug and alcohol abuse, and high dropout rates. Institutional bias and socioeconomic factors also play a huge role in the urban schools' failure to prepare African-American children. The result is that our school systems have produced a generation of many illiterates and underachievers. That explains why some student-athletes are not adequately prepared for the academic demands of college.

Possible Solutions: Short of revamping the entire public school system, our solutions revolve mainly around seeking outside assistance. The first step has to be recognizing that your school

Watson's Theory on Behaviorism and Shaping Intelligence

Give me a dozen healthy infants, and my own specified world to bring them up in, and I will make anyone of them into whatever I want them to be. I can shape them to be doctors, lawyers, beggars, and even thieves—regardless of their penchants, talents, and *the race of their ancestors.*

—John B. Watson (Founder of the Study of Behaviorism at the University of Chicago)

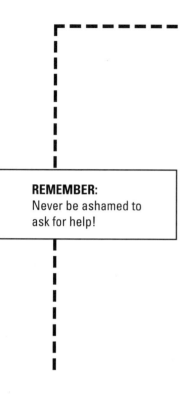

REMEMBER:
Never be ashamed to ask for help!

may be academically inadequate. Admitting that there is a problem will lead you to look for solutions. Say you have taken the SAT and your score reflects deficiencies in a particular area. The solution is to consider getting a tutor to help you improve. Although according to a recent admission on the part of the SAT Board the exam is culturally biased, it is important to remember that this test is still one of the gauges of academic ability. Thus, you have to achieve a good score for college admission. Once on campus, don't be ashamed to get help for areas in which you are having and/or have had difficulty.

7. Failure of universities to recognize the afore-mentioned factors. This failure on the part of some universities has led to a system that perpetuates the problem. As the saying goes, *"If you are not a part of the solution, then you are part of the problem."* In most cases, colleges have ignored or neglected the factors we have outlined. The fact that many of these problems surface daily in one form or another has done nothing to change the establishment's thinking. As previously mentioned, those factors are:

- Lack of familiar social circles
- Unrealistic expectations
- Coping with the components of racism
- Lack of community-based support
- Low self-esteem
- Failure of urban schools to provide adequate education

Possible Solutions: In order to change the attitude of the establishment, athletes and parents must become more vocal in demanding that this issue be dealt with. African-American student-athletes are failing to graduate at an alarming rate, and this problem can no longer be ignored. We cannot allow these institutions to come into our communities, take whatever commodities they need, and not consider the baggage that comes with the commodity. Each student-athlete's life and career expectations must be valued and seen as a potential resource for our communities. Parents and student-athletes must recognize that these problems exist, and take steps to counter them.

The Authors' Challenge

The majority of colleges refuse to institute policies to address the aforementioned problems, and some officials act as though social transitions for African-American student-athletes are not a serious problem.

We would like to challenge a contingent of college presidents, Boards of Regent members, college faculty, NCAA officials, and the like. The challenge is this: Send twenty such people on a little vacation, for say, thirty days. This vacation would be to places like Nickerson Gardens (Watts), Compton (California), Cabrini Green Housing Project (Chicago), Harlem (N.Y.), and The 5th Ward (Houston). All visitors would be required to stay in community-based housing. No special liaisons would be provided. Visitors would have to survive on their own. After thirty days, we guarantee that these people will realize the need for colleges toprovide adequate support systems for dealing with social transition problems. Anyone care to sign up?

Social Transition: Progress Self-Test

Formulated by Dr. Robert Sellers, University of Virginia Professor of Psychology

Quiz yourself on the success of your social transition via your academic, personal, and psychological progress. *Answer the following questions as honestly as you can. Each best answer is worth five points. See end of chapter for answer key.*

Academic Self-Test   (Circle the answer that best applies to you.)

1) **What is your overall G.P.A.?**
       a) 3.0- 4.0   b) 2.0-2.9   c) 1.0-1.9   d) 0.0-0.9

2) **Have you formally chosen or given serious thought to a particular field of study?**
       a) absolutely   b) occasionally   c) not seriously   d) not at all

3) **In what capacity was your major chosen?** Was it _____.
       a) your first choice   b) your second choice   c) out of desperation   d) not your choice;
                                                                         someone else made it

4) **What type of progress are you making toward your degree?**
       a) excellent   b) satisfactory   c) not satisfactory   d) none at all

5) **How much are you learning outside of the classroom (i.e., personally developing)?**
       a) learning a lot   b) slightly learning   c) learning little   d) not at all

6) **How informed are you of the academic commitment that your major involves?**
       a) well informed   b) fairly informed   c) slightly informed   d) uninformed

7) **How prepared are you to meet the challenge of that commitment?**
       a) extremely prepared   b) very prepared   c) slightly prepared   d) not prepared

Personal and Psychological Self-Test

1) **Are you satisfied with your college experience thus far?**
       a) very satisfied   b) somewhat satisfied   c) not satisfied   d) disappointed

2) **What is your overall opinion of yourself?**
       a) I think highly of myself   b) I think I'm an average guy   c) I am down on myself
       d) I haven't formulated an opinion of myself

3) **How often do you get depressed?**
       a) once a week   b) once a month   c) more than four times per month
       d) a few times a year

4) **If you could change schools without any penalties, would you do so?**
       a) absolutely   b) maybe   c) not sure   d) absolutely not

5) **Are you happy with the course that your life has taken?**
       a) yes   b) no   c) not sure   d) too early to tell

6) **Do you feel you have control over your life and future?**
       a) yes   b) no   c) not sure   d) haven't thought about it

7) **Have you experienced changes in your diet or sleep habits during times of stress?**
       a) less sleep/ more eating   b) more sleep/ more eating   c) less sleep/ less eating
       d) inconsistent patterns in sleeping and eating   e) no problems

Social Transition Progress Self-Test ANSWER KEY

Give yourself the maximum amount of points (five) for choosing the best answer. All other answers are scored based on how close they are to the best answer.

Academic Self-Test

1) a) 5 pts   b) 3 pts   c) 1 pt   d) 0 pts

2) a) 5 pts   b) 2 pts   c) 0 pts

3) a) 5 pts   b) 4 pts   c) 1 pt

4) a) 5 pts   b) 3 pts   c) 0   d) 0

5) a) 5 pts   b) 3 pts   c) 1 pt

6) a) 5 pts   b) 3 pts   c) 1 pt   d) 0

7) a) 5 pts   b) 4 pts   c) 2 pts

Personal and Psychological Self-Test

1) a) 5 pts   b) 4 pts   c) 0

2) a) 5 pts   b) 3 pts   c) 0   d) 0

3) a) 0   b) 3 pts   c) 0   d) 5 pts

4) a) 0   b) 0   c) 1 pt   d) 5 pts

5) a) 5 pts   b) 0   c) 2 pts   d) 3 pts

6) a) 5 pts   b) 0   c) 2 pts   d) 1 pt

7) Selection   a) - d) = 0 pts   e) 5 pts

About Dr. Robert Sellers

Dr. Robert Sellers is an expert on the life experiences of student-athletes. He has served as a consultant to the NCAA President's Commission Study of the Life Experiences of Student-Athletes. He is a member of the NCAA research committee, as well as the principal investigator of the Student-Athlete Life Stress Project.

Grading Scale

61-70 pts.......... Great job, keep doing what you're doing.

51-60 pts.......... Close, but not quite there yet. Find your weak link and fix it.

41-50 pts.......... Being average doesn't cut it. You need some assistance.

31-40 pts.......... Drastically alter your present course; you're going nowhere fast.

21-30 pts.......... Nowhere to go but up.

If you are in the top two scoring categories, you are to be commended. If you follow your present course, success is inevitable.

If you fall into any of the lower three scoring categories, you need to identify your problem(s). If your problem was covered in any of the seven basic problems, try following our suggested solutions. If that does not work, or if your particular problem is not listed, seek assistance from a mentor or coach. You can also contact us *(5A)* at 510-886-2415 for assistance.

NOTE:
We found this chapter to be especially challenging to write. It was therefore completed in consultation with Dr. Robert Sellers, Associate Professor of Psychology at the University of Virginia.

CHAPTER 5. ROAD WORK

A Manageable Approach to Academic Stardom

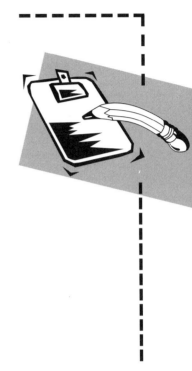

Few things that are worth pursuing happen without a plan. Take a touchdown, for example. In order for a team to score six points, the coach and his assistants have to come up with the most effective plays that the players then practice and later attempt to execute. If the team scores, that carefully orchestrated and carefully executed plan may look like an accident—to the untrained eye. Well, that's OK (see "Vince's Personal Time Management Strategy" in Chapter 6). What's important is that the plan worked. In this chapter, we'll help you figure out a plan for juggling the demands of college life.

Many courses and other books incorporate the steps we will discuss, but none address the issues from the standpoint of being an athlete and a student. Much of the information given by others is based on theory and other pseudo-scientific B.S. For example, some suggest using an all-purpose formula to tell you how many hours you should study per hour spent in class. This doesn't take into account that each person possesses varying levels of intelligence, time, desire, etc. We won't waste your time with such rigid guidelines. Instead, we will present some of the steps taken by present and former successful student-athletes. Use these suggestions, in addition to the skills you already have, in order to achieve the full benefit of attending an institute of higher education.

> One's work may be finished someday, but one's education, never.
>
> —Alexandre Dumas

Formulate a Plan

If the thought of designing your personal game plan terrifies you, don't sweat it. It's no great mystery. An academic game plan consists of the following elements:

Goals

This is all about deciding what you want. Don't worry about what methods you'll have to follow or the obstacles you may face. At this point, it's OK to dream.

Priorities

Decide the order in which you want to accomplish things. You can't have a strategy without order. Otherwise, you don't know when to do what.

Long-term objectives

Establish realistic and well-defined long-term objectives. By realistic, we mean that given who you are and the world around you, your goals aren't just possible, but also plausible. For example, if your goal is "to do well in school," your plan defines how you will do it. Remember, be specific. So, your long-term objectives might be some or all of the following:

- Graduate in four years and use my fifth year of eligibility for graduate studies, if I am redshirted.

- Graduate with a 3.5 G.P.A. or higher.

- Get accepted into business school upon completion of my general education requirements in my junior year.

Now it's your turn. Write three of your long-term objectives in the spaces below:

1. _____

2. _____

3. _____

Short-term objectives

If you plan to graduate, you can't do so without setting and meeting daily, weekly, or monthly objectives. Each class, study assignment, test, or internship that you complete is a short-term objective that helps turn your long-term objective into a measurable goal. And that was your plan all along.

Remember, a game plan should always be:

- Realistic
- Well-defined
- Exciting and meaningful, and most of all . . .
- *Implemented*

Choosing a Major

Used to be that you didn't have to decide on your major at the beginning of your college career. However, more and more institutions are structuring their degree programs in a way which forces you to choose early—if you hope to graduate in four years. This may account for the fact that students are taking, on average more than four years to graduate. But you may need to decide on a major to meet eligibility playing rules. The NCAA, in particular, has a rule dictating that you must declare a major:

NCAA Bylaw 14.4.3.1.4: This rule says that you must declare a major at the beginning of your third year. For schools on a quarterly schedule, your deadline is the seventh quarter; for those on a semester schedule, it's the fifth semester. If you don't declare, you won't be eligible to play until you start earning credits toward your major. It may not seem like it, but the intent of this rule is to help you work toward a degree, not punish you for being unsure about what you want to do.

What if you find yourself in a major that doesn't thrill you? Don't sweat it. You're not obligated for life. Business, industry, and government are full of people with degrees in history, sociology, and psychology, as well as those with specialized degrees. Plus, there is always the option of obtaining a postgraduate degree. What you need to remember is that the choice lies with you. The information below should aid you in making a decision.

GETTING STARTED

- Whether you know exactly what you want or do not have a clue, the best place to start working on your future is at your campus career center. In fact, it's more important for athletes to go this route than for any other group of students. At the career center are people who are not associated with the athletic department and are trained to guide your career choices. In other words, don't let the athletic department make career choices for you. That department's goal is to look out for the best interest of campus sports, not necessarily to chart your career.

- Most career centers offer some type of career placement tests. Take them. These tests are designed to identify your interests and basic ability. The results are interpreted by the career counselors and can identify careers that you might do well in. Do not base your entire future on these tests, but use them as a guide.

- While you're at the center, ask for information on what careers will be hot in the future. Don't assume that because a field is booming your freshman year that it will still be popular your senior year.

- Check out the school's course catalog. You may discover an area that you never considered, and you can use the career center to find out more about it.

- Don't let others, even your boys, set expectations for your academic success—especially ones that are too low. Some people are forever telling others what they can't do. Tell them to step off.

ONCE YOU HAVE AN IDEA

- Narrow your choices, then find out exactly what people in these fields do. Talk to people in the profession. Say your interest is in engineering. A call to the local chapter of the National Association for the Advancement of Colored People or the Urban League might lead you to the National Association of Black Engineers. Contact one of the officers in the organization and tell that person what you want to accomplish. Such a group should be more than willing to help you. In fact, many such organizations are looking to recruit people just like you.

- Talk to professors. Many of them have worked, or are still working, in the field you're considering. They should have the names of contact people they can pass along to you.

- Talk to students already accepted into the degree program. You probably know what we are going to say: Network, network, network. (See Chapter 10 for additional information.)

In other words, do whatever it takes to get a better understanding of a particular major as a student and as a member of the profession.

ONCE YOU DECIDE

- Do not rely on others to tell you what is required to graduate in your chosen major. We know one too many horror stories about people who relied on the word of others, only to find out they were short of the requirements to graduate. Now, wouldn't it be messed up to have your parents all excited to see you graduate—then find out that you can't?

- Seek help from academic guidance counselors, not the athletic department.

- Check for changes in the requirements for your major. Schools can revise requirements in an attempt to keep up with the demands of an ever changing employment world. You are responsible for keeping track of these changes.

- Competition for a spot in some of the more technical programs is intense. For these, you need to get your core courses out of the way as quickly as possible and, by all means, maintain a decent GPA.

- If you still manage to get into a major that is not for you, start looking into another one immediately. The sooner you make the change, the sooner you can adjust to a new field of study. Besides, wait too long and you might take a lot of unnecessary classes which will not count toward your new major.

CHOOSING CLASSES

Unlike high school, college offers a *cazillion* classes from which to choose. You'll be impressed by some. Others will seem like a major waste of time. Of course, some classes are requirements for graduation. For you, the student-athlete, developing a strategy for selecting classes will ease the struggle that comes with your dual role. In fact, in all decisions you make keep this thought in mind: *"Which choices will allow me to work smarter and not harder?"* Don't misunderstand us. We're not saying you should make a career out of taking easy classes. We just want you to get used to thinking smart. The following rules will assist you in working smarter, not harder.

RULE 1: Choose instructors, not classes

Pick classes based on who is teaching them, not for cute titles like "The Origin of Multiple Partner Sexual Relations." We can not overemphasize the effect a bad instructor can have on your ability and/or desire to learn, and ultimately your grades. Some instructors can be downright assholes! For example, one student-athlete had an instructor who proclaimed himself "Dr. Drop" because he made it a point to make students want to drop his classes. Now, why in the world would you want to have an instructor like this? Granted, sometimes these instructors do teach required classes and you'll just have to deal with them. Otherwise, do your homework. Choose instructors who have a reputation for being a "student's teacher." This is similar to the concept of a "player's coach." Good instructors are fair, understanding, and—most important—possess teaching skills. These professors are truly concerned about shaping young minds. The others might only be concerned with getting a paycheck or furthering research in their field.

RULE 2: Take less-intensive classes during the season

Naturally, the most time-consuming period of the academic year comes during the playing season. So why burden yourself with a bunch of reading-intensive or technical courses? Strive for a workable mix of classes. For example, take one or two reading-intensive classes along with some that are less challenging. In addition to easing the demands on your time, these classes can do wonders for your GPA. Then, take the more challenging classes in the off-season, when you have more time to devote to them.

RULE 3: Complete your General Education Requirements early

There are many horror stories about students who put off some of their general educational requirements until their senior year. Then when it was time to graduate, the classes were not available. Do not let this happen to you! Be smart and get these handled as soon as possible.

RULE 4: Don't sweat closed classes

You shouldn't worry too much if a class you really need (or maybe one you just want because a bunch of fly females are in it) is unavailable. Typically, all it takes to get in is some perseverance. Talk with the instructor or sit in on the class during the first few days, and you often can enroll once others drop the course. This strategy works best for getting into large, lecture-hall classes, but can also work with small ones, especially if you have established a relationship with the instructor.

RULE 5: Don't be a victim of "Weed-Out Classes"

Watch out for classes designed to separate those who are serious about a major from those who are not. For example, many schools require business majors to take beginning accounting classes. These classes are meant to be tough, thus causing people to re-evaluate their majors. These weed-out classes aren't always a true indication of how you'll handle the challenges of your particular major. The trick is to not let them defeat you and, by all means, not to use them as an excuse for failing.

RULE 6: Dropping a class can be beneficial

If you have enrolled in a class that is going to place your GPA in jeopardy, do not be afraid to drop it. It's also a good idea to consult your academic adviser. Realize, though, that this tactic may render you academically ineligible to compete in sports by reducing the class units you're required to have. If you have to drop a class, do it at the earliest possible moment. That way, you will be able to pick a substitute and maintain the required number of credits. One solution may be to take an independent studies class supervised by your favorite instructor. This option is far more likely to happen if you have developed a relationship with your instructors.

Classroom Etiquette

From the moment you step into a new class, many of you will be stereotyped by professors and students alike. You can assume that they are convinced of one thing: big Black guys only go to college to be athletes. Do not reinforce this stereotype by acting like the dumb jock. Instead, view yourself as a student, and demand that others view you that way, too. Here's how to communicate to the rest of the world that you are serious about getting an education:

FIRST IMPRESSIONS

- **Establish a name to go with your face** (i.e., make sure the professor knows your name).

- **Read the first assignment before the first day of class,** so that you can add to the classroom discussion. This is guaranteed to shock your professor and classmates.

- **Sit near the front of the room,** whenever possible. Everybody expects to find the smart, serious students at the head of the class. Why shouldn't you be there?

- **Ask questions.** If you're in a large, lecture-hall setting, approach the podium after class. In smaller settings, ask questions during class. The main reason for asking questions is to get noticed and show all that you are there to learn. Want to avoid feeling self-conscious? Like we said earlier, sit in the front row. This will give you a direct view of the professor— and you'll feel that fewer eyes are on you.

- **Visit instructors during office hours.** Get to know them, and give them the chance to learn more than your last name, Social Security number, and grades. Then, if you ever need to lobby for a better grade, the odds are better that the instructor will consider your appeal. That won't happen if you haven't laid the right groundwork. Instructors respect students who show an interest in learning.

CULTIVATE RELATIONSHIPS

- **Make as many friends as possible.** If you allow students to get to know you as a student, not just a Saturday hero, then they will begin to respect your academic abilities. Making friends will also come in handy if you miss class because of games. Your nonathlete friends may be willing to save much-needed class material for you.

- **Demand that people recognize you first as a student.** For example, limit the amount of time you let your classmates or professors talk to you about athletics. Talk about relevant classroom issues as much as possible; this will show everyone concerned that you are all about the business of education.

- **Don't allow others to set expectations for your academic success.** For example, if you have a group assignment, don't let others assume that you are not capable of writing the report or giving an oral presentation. If they suggest that you help gather the research, volunteer to help write the report or to do a part of the presentation. Then, do it better than anybody else.

BODY LANGUAGE

- **Make sure your posture doesn't betray you.** No matter how bored or tired you may be, sit up straight in your chair and focus on what's going on. Remember: people will be watching you.

As we said earlier, few things can be accomplished without some kind of game plan. Obviously, that includes attaining academic success.

CHAPTER 6. SMARTER, NOT HARDER

Study Skills

You already know that certain skills are required to be competitive in sports. Competing academically is no different. You can't play this "game" either if you don't have the right skills. What's different about these two forms of competition is the results.

Once you've finished battling on the collegiate field or on the court, you might—or might not—have something to show for your efforts. If you're exceptional, you'll be drafted. If you remain exceptional, you'll have a shot at a lucrative career. If you stay healthy, you'll reap some serious benefits. In each phase of this scenario, you'll face steep odds, intense competition, and other factors that could hinder you from entering this small pool of talented people.

On the other hand, your academic pursuits yield different results. Once you've completed your major, the value of your degree will remain constant. Exceptional people still rule in the nonathletic world, but since the pool is so large, the odds against success, the competition, and other factors are far less.

Look at it this way: earning a college degree means that you won't end up as a benchwarmer in the nonathletic world. Your education guarantees you a shot at competing—and succeeding—in your chosen field. Of course, none of this will happen if you don't hit the books in school. That means you can't afford to look at studying as some horrific evil that you must endure in order to remain eligible. See it as part of the processes for lifelong success, and *take pride* in doing your best.

> Education remains the key to both economic and political empowerment.
>
> —Barbara Jordan

Your personal study techniques will evolve and improve over time as you determine what works and what doesn't. We offer the following to point you in the right direction.

Getting Your Head in the Game

Before you start cracking the books, you'll need to get your head in the game. Here's what you'll need to get started.

Take Responsibility and Don't Make Excuses

Step up and take responsibility for your own success. Try to limit your mistakes, but when one is made, learn from it and move on. Minorities can come up with many legitimate excuses for failure, but few people care. Had Andre used his South Central upbringing as an excuse to fail, his family might have cared, but that is about as far as it would have gone. So why make excuses? Just get the job done. As the legendary Coach Vince Lombardi once said, "An obstacle is what you see when you take your eye off of the road."

Manage Your Emotions

Emotional distractions can throw you off your most well-prepared game plan. Learn to manage your emotions and take pride in not allowing other people and circumstances to adversely affect them. Have you ever been excited about something only to have someone react negatively and kill your enthusiasm? What about the important exam you were studying for just prior to getting into it with your girl? These are the types of situations you want to effectively manage.

Achieving emotional stability isn't easy, but through practice it is possible. Here's how:

- Put problems in perspective. As bad as things might seem, it's a sure bet that they could be worse.

- Set aside negative feelings until you are able to deal with them. (If you are stressed about something which is unrelated to the final exam you have on Friday, try not to think about the problem until Saturday.)

- Take pride in not allowing others to adversely affect your emotions.

- Develop a form of relaxation that you find enjoyable and effective (i.e., yoga, meditation, Sega, music, cooking, etc.).

- If all else fails, seek professional help from a therapist. That's right, a therapist. Emotional problems are your mind's way of saying that your life is out of order. As odd as it may seem, sometimes it takes an outsider to guide you through your personal maze. Usually, that kind of help is available on campus for no charge. Don't consider it a weakness to take advantage of this service.

Seek Academic Assistance

When it comes to matters of academics, try to seek as much outside counseling and guidance as possible from the people that nonathletes turn to for help. These people will have few incentives or pressures to steer you down the wrong path. Getting to know and relying on these people will also make you feel more a part of the general student body, which is something many athletes complain about.

Create a Suitable Study Environment

Whether you are the type of person who can study while everyone around you is raising hell, or you need total silence, you need to find an environment that's ideal for studying. This is a place where you won't be distracted from your assignments. College campuses have a vast number of nooks and crannies; find the right spot for yourself.

Increase Your Reading Speed

Reading consumes a major part of a college student's time; slow reading makes things even worse. It can contribute to a student's low grades and lack of interest in classes. In college you will be responsible for reading tons of textbooks, novels, even magazines. Imagine dragging yourself to your dorm after practice. It's already 7 p.m., and you have to read two boring, thirty-plus page psychology chapters, a forty-five page math chapter, and also get up to date on current events for macroeconomics (and you read at a snail's pace). Such a reading load is not uncommon in college, so prepare yourself. Numerous books and courses will help you get through this.

Conquering Concepts

Here's how the educational process usually works. Students go to class and take notes. At exam time, they memorize a bunch of information that they regurgitate onto a piece of paper. By the next day, they have forgotten ninety percent of the information. It doesn't have to be this way. While scoring well on exams is extremely important, it's more important to understand the concepts you are being tested on and to be able to utilize them. If you decide that you really want to understand the "why" and "how" of concepts, good grades will follow. That's because you remember concepts a lot longer than answers. Here's what we mean. Pretend that you are a first grader and your teacher asks, "What is two times five?" You answer ten because you memorized it. (Lucky for you, because it was the only one you memorized.) Your teacher says, "Good! Since you did so well with that one, what is four times five?" Uh oh. This one you neglected to memorize. Your guess is twenty-six. Had you understood the concept that multiplication is actually a form of addition, then you could have at least counted on your fingers: $5 + 5 + 5 + 5 = 20$. With that said, let's move on.

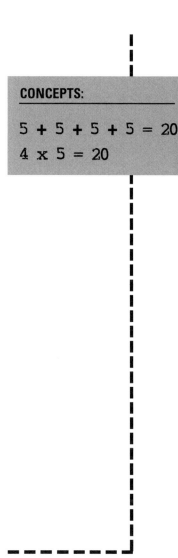

CONCEPTS:

$5 + 5 + 5 + 5 = 20$

$4 \times 5 = 20$

Taking Notes

Note taking is a personal thing. No one else's notes can compare to yours. Of course, you can't have your own notes if you don't attend class—often. Plus, attending class implants images and sounds in your head which can spark your memory during an exam. Some key things to remember when taking notes:

- Read the assigned material prior to going to class. This will help you follow the lecture and hopefully make it more interesting. At the very least, read the chapter summaries.
- Try to limit your note taking to the important concepts. Be aware of clues as to what is important, such as:
  - the vocal emphasis an instructor places on a particular subject
  - concepts being listed in some type of order

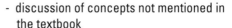

- discussion of concepts not mentioned in the textbook
- the use of visual aids to emphasize points

- Record notes in your textbooks. After all, you've paid for them. Some people suggest using a highlighter to mark important areas; others favor putting notes on a separate sheet of paper. Determine what works best for you.

- Finally, if you are still unsure of what is most important, ask the instructor. You might be surprised at how much information he/she is willing to divulge.

Rewriting Notes. Some people believe that rewriting or typing your notes is necessary for retaining information. We strongly disagree, for these reasons:

- As an athlete, your time is already limited time; you can't devote more of it to this futile activity. The time you invest outweighs the potential benefits.

- Your original notes, along with the sights and sounds experienced while taking them, can aid dramatically in your recall of the material. For example, have you ever started doodling (drawing pictures of monsters, cars, etc.) on your notes while in class? Later, as you reviewed the notes and saw the doodling, you were able to recall what was discussed that day.

Reviewing Notes. Experts and nonexperts agree that constantly reviewing your material will help increase retention and ultimately cut down on test preparation time.

EXAM PREPARATION

One of the best attitudes you can have when preparing for an exam is to see it as a dogfight. In order to do your best; you are going to have to bite, kick, and claw for every point. In other words, short of outright cheating, just about everything else goes. Throughout the grading period, your goal should be to learn and absorb the course material. Exam time is for collecting points that will follow you (by way of your transcript) for the rest of your life. Some of the suggestions that follow should help you claw your way to the top:

- If the instructor doesn't tell you what the exam will cover, <u>ask</u>.

- Get copies of old exams in order to get an idea of the material being tested. A good place to start your search for old exams is in the frats. Many fraternities keep test files of old exams for their members, and it's up to you to befriend members so that you will have access.

- Make a study schedule and stick to it. (See Chapter 5.)

- Participate in study groups. They often shed new light on class material.

- Formulate a logical flow of the material being covered for a particular exam period. Establish an overall view of how the various concepts, formulas, time periods, etc. fit together. Understanding the logical flow or purpose of the material can aid you in answering questions not specifically covered in class or in the reading material.

- Develop a system for memorizing necessary materials. Yeah, we know we've made memorization seem like a bad word, but sometimes it is necessary. If you are seriously interested in improving your memory, explore some techniques that might be suitable for you (i.e., flash cards, word association, acronyms).

- Utilize tutors provided by the athletic department and/or school.

Cramming

If you fail to follow your beautifully conceived study plan, then you had better know a little about cramming.

- Act with urgency, but *don't panic.* The exam you are facing is just one of many you will take in your lifetime. Please don't get carried away with this logic to the point where there are no more exams left to take.

- Stock up on your favorite pick-me up drink and junk food to keep you going while you study; it will be a long night.

- At this point, you still have to have a plan. It should include tackling the more difficult information first. You might even want to gamble and disregard areas you doubt will be on the exam.

- Find a place to study where the temptation to fall asleep is limited. More than likely, you brought this necessity upon yourself due to procrastination, so deal with it.

- Just prior to taking the test, review your notes—especially in the areas you spent little time on. This will help you retain the material for the duration of the exam.

REMEMBER:
Next time, don't put yourself in a cramming predicament.

EXAM-TAKING TIPS

College exams typically fall into two categories: essay and/or multiple choice. We will address strategies for doing well on each, as well as some general exam taking techniques.

Essay Exams

1. Prior to the exam, make sure that you are familiar with all of the "buzzwords" related to the subject, especially the ones used by the instructor or in the textbook. Think of these words as the lingo used by those who are in this field of study. The words will be the glue that holds your essay in place.

2. Read the questions carefully, then formulate an outline making sure that all parts of the question are addressed. It will save time if your make your outline directly on your answer booklet, then simply fill in the body of it. You will receive a better grade if the grader reads an effectively organized answer.

3. Answer in clear, precise sentences. No instructor will be fooled or impressed by a bunch of rambling B.S.

4. When including broad generalizations in your answer, support them with relevant examples or details. This tactic is often the difference between an average and an above-average grade.

5. Attempt to answer all questions. This is a good time to start throwing out more of the buzzwords we talked about. You might get partial credit.

6. Budget your time based on the possible point value of individual questions. If the exam is only fifty-five minutes long and there are four questions, one worth ten points and the other three worth thirty points each, don't spend the first thirty minutes working on the ten point question.

7. If time permits, check all of your answers. Look for areas where you can grab extra points.

Multiple Choice

These exams are usually time intensive. They could be sixty minutes long and include sixty questions. Naturally, you do not have much time to spend on any one question. The key to passing these tests is budgeting your time. Also keep these points in mind:

1. Multiple choice answers which include the words "always," "never," or "absolutely" are usually wrong.

2. Statistics have shown that your first response is often the correct one. Think twice about changing your first response.

3. Try to eliminate obvious wrong answers and make an educated guess on the remainder.

General Techniques

1. During the exam, ask the instructor to rephrase a question you do not quite understand. The response may give you a subtle hint as to the answer.

2. It is never too late to lobby for a higher grade, even after you've taken the test. Make sure you go over your missed questions thoroughly. Sometimes, an instructor or an assistant makes mistakes or doesn't understand your answer.

Lobbying for a better grade is a prime opportunity to show the professor that you are genuinely concerned about your education. It also allows you to verbally demonstrate knowledge of the material, which may pay dividends. It's best to approach an instructor during office hours, not in front of others during class. Don't be confrontational. This will definitely decrease your chances for success. By following this approach, you will more than likely get a few extra points, if not this time, then down the road.

3. Tell your instructor that you absolutely have to get a certain grade in the class and ask if there is anything extra that you can to do to get it. (And no, sex is out of the question.) If the answer is yes, seize the opportunity. If not, at least the instructor knows your level of commitment to the class. That could be an advantage at final grading time. If you find yourself on the borderline between the 3.2 you want and a 3.14, there is a better chance you might get the 3.2 if you speak to the instructor.

Term Papers and Reports

During your college career, you will be assigned several term papers and reports. Here's what you need to know to get the job done.

Start Early. Term papers and reports, like tests, are the staples of college life. They cannot be avoided, but they can be managed. Instructors will let you know at the beginning of the grading period if reports or term papers are required. Advance notice is your biggest ally. If ever there was a time not to procrastinate, this is it. Writing a thirty-page report the day before it is due is plain stupid.

REMEMBER:
You *can* study on a beautiful sunny day if you realize that it will always be sunny somewhere, and by studying *now* you will have the means to go there.

the sport of learning

Choosing a Topic. Your instructor will probably allow some discretion in choosing a topic. If at all possible, choose an area that interests you or one you know something about. Once you have a topic, you should narrow or expand it to fit the required length of the report. For example if your paper is supposed to be ten to twelve pages and the general topic is "American Wars," you probably don't want to talk about every last one of them. You might want to narrow your topic to "American Wars of the 1900s." If the paper needs to be longer, expand the topic. Make sure the topic is defined well enough to coincide with the length of your paper so that you won't be "talking loud and saying nothing."

Do Not Plagiarize. In case you don't know, plagiarism means biting word for word from someone else's work and not giving them credit. If plagiarism is discovered, it could lead to a failing grade, suspension, or expulsion. Many people will expect you, the athlete, to do this because they don't believe you are capable of doing the work. Prove them wrong.

Avoid Big Words. Do not waste your time thinking that because you are in college, you are expected to use big words that most people do not understand. Professors are not impressed by someone who obviously used a thesaurus to change perfectly acceptable words into long, convoluted phrases.

Presentation. Even if you can not type or do not own a computer, make sure that any paper you turn in is done on a computer. Presentation may not be everything, but it does have merit. And make sure your paper is free of spelling and grammatical errors. Just because some cute woman typed it, don't assume that she was conscientious or that she writes better than you. Before you write a final draft of your paper, ask a tutor to review it and help you make changes in substance, grammar, etc.

Miscellaneous

Here is a bunch of stuff that should be useful in all aspects of your academic endeavors:

- Concentrate in order to maximize your time.
- Take frequent short breaks in order to sustain concentration.
- Plan a reward for yourself for completion of your daily tasks.
- In your spare time, read . . . read . . . read! It will make you a better student.
- Work to increase your vocabulary.
- **Remember:** you can study on a beautiful sunny day if you realize that it will always be sunny somewhere, and by studying *now* you will have the means to go there.

notes:

CHAPTER 7. WORKING THE CLOCK

The Art Of Getting Things Done

Mama sure knows how to get things done, doesn't she? Just think about what she does to get everybody up and on their way in the morning. Up before dawn, she makes sure everybody else stumbles out of bed. Then she keeps everybody moving, checking to see if you finally made it out the bathroom and if your sister actually picked out something to wear. (She'd better if she doesn't want Mama to do it.) By the time your school bus arrives, everybody has been fed and reminded of some important piece of information they'll need that day. And somehow, Mama has managed to get herself dressed in time to leave the house. Do you know another adult who can manage things like Mama can?

Well, once you set foot on campus, you will automatically be considered an adult. At that point, you alone will face demands and obligations from all directions. Only then will you appreciate what Mama did for you all those years. Everyone from coaches and professors to classmates will be demanding a part of you. You're probably wondering, "How in the hell am I going to go to class, work out, hang with the fellas, check out the honeys, go to practice, eat dinner, meet with a study group, go to the library, shoot to my girl's crib, and play a game of Sega all in one day?" The bottom line is: if you don't get a grip on time, you won't be able to do much of anything, and academic and athletic success may be very elusive. Self-discipline and a game plan will do wonders in helping you meet all the demands in

> Time is life. It is irreversible and irreplaceable. To waste your time is to waste your life, but to master your time is to master your life and make the most of it.
>
> —Alan Lakein

your life. (Obviously, Mama couldn't make it without them.) The following suggestions should aid you in managing time:

Getting a Grip on Time

1. As with any plan, you must first identify your objectives and the factors which affect the outcome. The factors vary, depending on your priorities, but typically fall into three categories:

- Class obligations: reports, exams, group sessions, labs, homework

- Team obligations: practice, meetings, treatment, weights, games

- Social obligations: relationships, leisure, sleep

Write down the general factors affecting your objectives in the space below.

General Factors

_____

_____

_____

_____

_____

_____

2. Once the general factors are identified, you need to gather information in order to come up with specific factors. You should quantify your specific factors in terms of times and dates. For example, you need to determine the date of your sociology midterm, how much time you need to prepare for it, and how your other obligations might conflict. Some of the tools you will need are:

- A calendar with boxes large enough to write in
- A course syllabus: this is an outline of the course material and includes assignments, and times and dates of exams and papers
- Team material: information about practice, game, and meeting schedules as well as other important dates and times
- Other stuff of interest: holiday functions, concerts, fairs, etc.

Spend the next day or two gathering the necessary information to construct your game plan. Yeah, we know this sounds a little elementary, but it works.

3. After you have completed Step 2, use a large calendar to record daily and weekly goals that you will follow to the best of your ability. Planning your time this way enhances your chances of getting things done and forces you to be realistic about what you can—or can't—do.

Example:
Monday, October 22, 1999, might look like this:

7:45 A.M.	Treatment	2:00	Meeting
8:30	Geography	3:30	Practice
9:30	Economics	7:30	Group Study
10:30	Afram	8:30	Break
11:30	Lunch	9:00	Private Study
1:00 P.M.	Treatment	12:30 A.M.	Lights Out

Sit down with your information and plot a general schedule for the entire semester or quarter. This will be your game plan, but realize that it is subject to change. It will get you thinking about things you will have to do in the not-so-distant future. You should also do a more detailed schedule, which breaks down either the following week or month. This is the plan that you will use on a daily basis to help you better utilize the hours in the day. When finished, put your schedule someplace where you can review it daily.

Below is a list of general time-saving strategies from former student-athletes:

- Use downtime, such as treatment sessions, to also knock out some studying.

- Make sure your schedule is flexible so that it won't become monotonous.

- Incorporate some leisure time into your schedule.

- Reward yourself for successfully completing scheduled tasks.

- Concentrate on what you're doing so you can get the maximum results.

- Set your watch a few minutes fast to keep yourself ahead of schedule.

- Don't allow others to throw you off your schedule.

- Make a daily to-do list of things that aren't on your master schedule.

- Stay focused on your priorities.

- Take pride in being on time and fulfilling your commitments.

- Make only commitments which you have a reasonable chance of keeping.

- Believe that your plan will achieve the desired results.

COLORED PEOPLE'S TIME (CPT)

Before ending this chapter we, would like to leave you with one last thought. We are sure that you are aware of the acronym CPT, but forget that you have ever heard of it. We want you to know that we despise everything about this characterization. For years, Black folks have been characterized as shiftless, lazy, and unreliable. Although we don't deserve to be stigmatized this way, these traits are all in line with the concept of CPT.

CPT is all about wasting opportunity. What do we mean by that? Well, say you're up for a job interview. You've already been through the process one too many times—and you're

Vince's Personal Time Management Strategy

While in school, some of my teammates use to think that I was da bomb because I drank Forties (See Chapter 12, Almost Addicted), chased women, and hung out while—at the same time—maintaining a relatively high GPA. Believe me, my success was not due to me being da bomb, but to self-discipline and organization. I had a game plan which was designed to make people think that I always had time for leisure. I have never shared this before, because I want my boys to continue thinking I'm the shit, but I will share it with you. My plan consisted of completing class assign-ments in advance. I mean *way* in advance. The first week of each quarter I would review my syllabi and plot my strategy, a strategy most conducive to reading-intensive classes. During the first few weekends of the quarter I would spend Saturday and Sunday, from 10 a.m. to 6 p.m., reading, doing home-work, and taking good notes on as many chapters as I could. Typically, I was able to do three to four chapters per weekend. I did this until I had completed all of the reading and homework for the quarter, which took only two to three weeks to complete. This left me with approximately seven to eight weeks in a ten-week quarter to concentrate on my other classes, which were usually less intense. A few early mornings of sacrifice would leave me with weeks of unpres-sured time to hang out. At exam time, I simply reviewed my notes and homework. My particular strategy worked best in the off-season, but I hope you can see how it can be applied at other times.

still unemployed. No doubt you're discouraged, if not outright pissed, and you see no reason to haul ass in order to make this appointment on time. You know the outcome. In fact, you've already determined it. From the moment you decided not to show up on time, you were screwed. Why? Because the manager in the position of hiring you does not tolerate CPT. He can't afford to operate that way; he's got deadlines to meet and a boss (which, by the way, you don't have until you find a job) to please. So that manager will use your lack of punctuality to rule you out as a job candidate. You know what his rationale is? *Why should I hire this fool? He's already wasting my time and he doesn't even work here.* Regardless of what this person thinks of you, the worst thing is that you're still out of a job. Now do you see why they say time is money?

There is absolutely nothing cute about wasting time. Just ask any sister who's been stood up. By the time you show up, she goes off—and she should. Among other things, she's going to let you know that her time is too valuable to waste on your sorry butt. That's how you should be when somebody subjects you to CPT. Let them know not to waste your time.

Student-athletes, whose free time is practically nonexistent, can ill afford to waste it. In fact, successful student-athletes should be the most disciplined people on campus. That, of course, fuels their success. But if you're not practicing punctuality and time management *today,* don't expect to suddenly grasp these concepts in college. Punctuality and time management are assets that will serve you well throughout your life, whether you are in the locker room or the boardroom. Now is the time to get used to them.

Food for Thought:

If time is money and you like money, why would you ever be late?

Structured Diplomacy

Personality Conflicts: How to Work Through Them

Throughout your life, you will be involved in numerous social interactions, some positive and some negative. Therefore, it is of the utmost importance that you develop a good understanding of human nature, and realize that all people will not get along all of the time. Once you understand this, you may learn not to take personality conflicts so personally, and develop the ability to work through them. The ability to work with people with whom you clash is a major accomplishment. However, the highest accomplishment in this area is not just the ability to get by, but *to progress* in not-so-friendly situations.

> **REMEMBER:**
> Business is never personal.

PERCEPTIONS

Perceptions play a huge role in whether you successfully get along with other people. There will be times when you might do something that you intend to be taken a certain way, but your actions will be perceived in a totally different light. This lack of a clear understanding on both sides can often lead to conflict. Therefore, it is important for you to understand the mentality of the people you are dealing with so that you can better anticipate how your actions will be perceived. For example, you might want to wear a

The essence of politics is power, and power can be defined as the social capacity to realize one's will even in opposition to others.

—Maulana Karenga

"do rag" on your head when you go to class because that is what you are used to doing. Your intent is not to look like a thug, but to get your hair to act right. Your classmates may see this and think that you are in some sort of gang. Yes, this is an unfair stereotype, but it is also an example of how others' perceptions are not always in line with your intent.

DIPLOMACY

The ability to be diplomatic (i.e., showing sensitivity and skill in dealing with others) is one of the keys to success. Anyone can excel in a friendly environment, but to excel under hostile circumstances is something that not everyone can do. For example, throughout history there have been times where two countries were at the brink of conflict. Moments before the first bullet was fired, one diplomat intervenes to find common ground, and saves thousands of lives in the process. This is diplomacy at its finest. The ability to focus on both sides and bring the two sides to resolution (i.e., to find common ground) is a skill not everyone can master. *Understanding both sides of the issue is the essence of diplomacy.*

A Lesson in Diplomacy: The Missiles of October and the Brink of Nuclear Conflict

In the summer of 1962, U-2 reconnaissance flights over Cuba showed evidence of missile sites under construction. When confronted with these facts, the Russians denied knowledge of any missile sites. President John F. Kennedy ordered a blockade of the entire island until the missile sites were dismantled and removed. Soviet President Krushchev publicly continued to deny the presence of any Soviet missile sites in Cuba.

On October 19, 1962, at least twenty-five Soviet merchant ships, some no doubt loaded with intermediate-range missiles, were steaming toward Cuba, and a confrontation with the American fleet was inevitable. For nine days, the world held its breath as we came to the brink of nuclear conflict. If those ships had been stopped and searched by the U. S. Navy, war would have been inevitable. Finally, after heavy negotiations, Kennedy was able to get Krushchev to turn the ships around and withdraw the missile sites. The Soviet ships were less than three hours from Cuba when they were ordered to turn back. The diplomacy and resolve showed by the Kennedy Administration in the face of nuclear conflict has been unparalleled in the history of this nation.

TWO SIDES OF THE SAME STORY

In any interactive relationship, both parties have to be accountable for what happens during the course of the relationship, whether the interaction is positive or negative. When there is tension or disagreement, no one side can be held solely accountable for the conflict. As the saying goes, "It takes two to tango." In the following section, we will discuss player/coach relationships from both sides of the fence.

Coaches

Coaching sports on any level can be a difficult task, but the immense pressure felt on the collegiate level is unparalleled in the world of sports. Colleges can only recruit, not draft, players. Unlike in the pros, colleges are not allotted a shot at the premiere players after a losing season. Consequently, losing programs have a hard time attracting marquee players.

During your college career, you might encounter a coach you do not get along with. In some cases this is perfectly normal, because in life you will not get along with everyone you meet. However, it is imperative that you develop the insight necessary to work through these potential conflicts. We surveyed several Division I assistant ccaches, and posed a list of questions. Their answers should give you some insight as to why a coach might act a certain way, and how you can effectively deal with these problems. The respondents spoke to us on the condition that we not identify them by name.

Sport of Learning: *Why do some coaches play mind games with their players?*

COACH: Mental preparation is a part of any sport. Oftentimes, we test players' mental ability to deal

REMEMBER:
Your intentions are only as good as how they are perceived.

with adverse situations. For example, if we are unsure about the mental maturity of a player, we might gauge his response to things that don't go his way. If a player loses his cool just because he doesn't get his way, I have to ask myself if this is someone I could count on in the heat of battle.

S. O. L.: *Why do coaches seem to like players who spend a lot of extra time before and after practice preparing for a game?*

COACH: Anyone in this profession will naturally be drawn to a player who not only wants to play, but wants to win, and who has a deep desire to do whatever it takes to win. Being well studied and drilled only make for a better player, and good players make us coaches look good.

S. O. L.: *Why do some coaches tell you one thing, then do something else?*

COACH: Coaches are human beings, too, who make mistakes just like anybody else. However, we are put in the precarious position of having to keep up the morale of our players win, lose, or draw. Sometimes we promise things that we can't deliver, but it is with good intentions. At times I might have a truly difficult time keeping my word, and changes (such as playing time) may take longer than I expected. But I feel like if you have a kid who is talented, at some point you have to give him some projection on when he might be playing, in order to keep his hopes up.

S. O. L.: *Why do some coaches say bad things about their players in staff meetings?*

COACH: I don't think it is so much that they say bad things. Oftentimes, they give their true opinion of a player. My philosophy is that I refuse to cover up the mistakes of a player and jeopardize my job. I work hard at what I do, and I don't want to be perceived as being the problem when I am not. So if a player screws up, then I make him solely accountable for his actions. People often forget that we have families to feed and bills to pay, and if we don't do a good job, we will be looking elsewhere for work. I would say that there is probably a very small percentage of incidents where a coach unjustly blames a player. A good head coach will make sure that a player gets fair and equitable treatment.

S. O. L.: *Why do some coaches divulge information to others after they were sworn to secrecy?*

COACH: In all honesty, the best way to keep a secret is to keep it to yourself. Controversial information can be like a big weight hanging around your conscience. Sometimes, what happens is that a kid will share something in confidence, then after the fact the coach makes a decision based on one or two things: 1) The information is too important or potentially dangerous to keep to himself; or 2) If he doesn't tell and the situation worsens, and anyone finds out that he knew about this problem and kept quiet, he could lose his job. In most cases, no secret is worth risking your job, or the personal safety of one of your kids.

S. O. L.: *As a player, what are your options when you have a problem with a coach?*

COACH: 1) Don't ever get physically confrontational; it will only get you kicked off the team and maybe out of school. If you need to verbally vent your frustrations, we recommend that you do this in the privacy of his office.

2) When something is bothering you, immediately set up a meeting with the head coach so that the problem doesn't fester and get worse.

3) If the problem is with the head coach, meet with him privately to discuss the issues. Try to understand what his intentions are; you may find that they are a lot different from your perceptions. Keep the lines of communication open at all times.

4) If your differences cannot be resolved, maybe there is a communication problem. Have an elder become your spokesperson (i.e., father, mother, uncle, or high school coach), and try to find out what the communication problem is. It may be a situation where you and your coach are not hearing each other, and a mediator may be necessary to get both points across. *This may work in either situation, whether the problem is the coach or the player.*

5) If your differences cannot be resolved after a reasonable and extensive number of attempts, then you should consider finding another school. Although these types of situations are rare, you must recognize this as an option. If you have exhausted the above steps, chances are that you have not alienated your coaches. Thus, they may not make it difficult for you to transfer (i.e., release you).

Not My Kind of Coach

Coming into my final season, I felt pretty good about my career. I had a pretty good junior year, and my expectations for my senior year were even greater. However, during the off-season, a funny thing happened: my position coach left, and they hired a new guy. Right away, there was a personality conflict. His first comment to me was, "I saw some film of you, and if you play like that for me, then you won't be playing." So right away I recognized there was a potential problem, but I did not let it deter me. I blocked out as much of his negativity as I could, and focused on developing my skills and taking care of business. *This is what separates players from nonplayers: the ability to be mentally tough. The game is as much mental as it is physical, so you have to be prepared in both areas in order to succeed.* I recognized that he was the coach, and that he had the upper hand. So I figured that if I would concentrate and just perform, then he would have to play me. After all, it was his job to field the best team possible. The coach ended up platooning me, which hurt my professional stock tremendously. I didn't even get drafted, and had to go free agent But *I STILL MADE IT!* Played in the league for eight years. All because I persevered, remained focused, kept my confidence, and didn't let the personality conflicts get to me. Now if I saw him today, *well I just might *%@*~*%@ and beat the # out of him.*

—J. P., Class of '85

Player Attitudes

As you go through your career as a student-athlete, you may find yourself in a situation where a particular coach perceives you or one of your teammates as having an attitude problem. In some cases the player's intent may be wrongly perceived by the coach; in others the player in question may actually have an attitude problem. Let's look at some possible examples of a player's actions and intentions versus a coach's perceptions.

Player Action	Intent	Coach's Perception
Wears bandanna or 'do rag	To keep his hair waved	Gang affiliation, hoodlum looking, bad image for program
Wears a lot of jewelry (i.e., earrings, necklaces)	To look sharp, trendy; likes the way it looks	Trying to be a show-off, drawing much attention to self, and where did he get the money to buy it?
Tests the rules regarding facial hair or hair style by not shaving or cutting hair	To avoid dealing with skinproblems related to shaving or cutting hair	Trying to buck the system, trouble maker, rebellious
Doesn't move quickly between drills at practice	Trying to be cool, feeling tired, just isn't a practice player	Disrespectful, lazy, not disciplined, lacks desire
Plays rap music extremely loud in dorms, car stereo, or with headphones	Trying to get pumped for practice, game, or just his way of coping	Being disruptive, acting with no class, acting thuggish; sees rappers encouraging violence
Seems too laid back during practice or a game mentally (i.e., not cheerleading)	Might not be cheerleader, may be into the game, within himself	Not a team player, disinterested, doesn't have head into game
Wears African attire or has Afrocentric name	Proud of his heritage and culture, politically aware	Radical, militant, divisive, or controversial

We accept the fact that social and cultural differences often exist between coaches and student-athletes, and as a result the actions of the African-American student-athlete can be misconstrued. It is our intent to provide you and your coaches with some insight in this area, and move toward closing the gap that often exists between coach and student-athlete. When you recognize perception to be the problem, sit down with your coach and explain where you are coming from. Also, try to understand his concerns as a coach. The sharing of information will help to alter people's perceptions.

BAAAD ATTITUDES

Although student-athletes by and large have good attitudes, there is a small yet significant group of you who do have attitude problems.

The question for you then becomes: "How do I identify whether I have an attitude problem?" The following information may assist you in making that determination.

Check Yourself Before You Wreck Yourself!

You might be the problem if...

You get called into the coach's office so often you memorize his picture arrangements.

You get into frequent confrontations with teammates, other students, roommates, and anyone else you come in contact with.

You have a "F— the coach" mentality.

You walk around with a chip on your shoulder, thinking it's you against the world.

You think that no one can tell you anything.

You are convinced it is *always* somebody else's fault.

You get into frequent trouble with campus authorities, law enforcement officers, and other authority figures.

You get called in by your coach and he says, "*You* need an attitude adjustment". (This may be based partly on fact, partly on perception.)

You are frequently misread by people, who later tell you that they initially thought you were an asshole.

Attitude Adjustments

In any environment where your behavior is being evaluated, it is important that you get regular feedback from the person evaluating you. This is not only true when dealing with coaches, but in the work force as well. The following information gives you some parameters for correcting attitude problems you might have, either real or perceived.

1. Use good judgment. You know right from wrong, so stop doing stupid things that get you into trouble, and stay out of the coach's office (unless you want to be there). Also, avoid people you know to be troublemakers.

2. Learn when and where to be confrontational. There is a time and place for everything. Leave the tough guy attitude on the field. Don't be confrontational with people you have to deal with every day. If you are not sure what behavior is acceptable, ask some of the highly respected veterans on the team, or one of the graduate assistants.

3. Get rid of the "F— the coach" mentality. Never forget who is in charge. A coach can be your sweetest dream or your worst nightmare. F— the coach? Fine, then watch the coach say, "F— you," too. Let's see who comes up on the short end.

4. Dealing with the law. In his book *Two Nations*, Professor Andrew Hacker states that "one out of every five Black men will spend some part of his life behind bars." Obviously, this means that an even greater percentage will have a negative encounter with the law that doesn't necessarily lead to incarceration. We would be remiss if we didn't attempt to give you some guidelines on dealing with this if it occurs. (See page 117 for tips.)

5. Be a good citizen. Remember that as a student-athlete, you are under a microscope. If you so much as spit on the sidewalk, it makes the news. Make a conscious effort to maintain a clean image, stay far away from trouble.

6. Listen to your coach. If your coach perceives you as having an attitude, then make the effort to either change your attitude or change his perception. This can be done through open communication between you and your coach, and through your developing a better understanding of what he expects of you.

7. Champion a spokesperson. Choose your old high school coach, your parents, or an uncle. Have them act as a mediator between you and your coach. Sometimes, you might shut down and not listen to your coach, but you might be more apt to listen to a relative or mentor. On the other hand, your coach just might be willing to listen to someone "older and wise."

Tips For Dealing With Police Officers

Remain Calm: This will allow you to make good decisions which could make the difference between life and death.

Be Extremely Polite: Some officers look for any excuse to go upside your head. While we recognize that some people see politeness as a weakness, this tactic will more often prove beneficial.

Be Very Cooperative: The side of a dark road is not the time to wage a battle with people who have badges, guns, and the law on their side. Follow the officers' instructions as best you can.

Refrain from Sudden Moves: With the level of violence that exists in our world, it is no wonder that officers tend to be nervous. This may cause them to act overly aggressive in dealing with what they see as potentially dangerous situations. Nervous people are prone to have accidents; do your part to avoid being the victim of such an accident.

Quickly Establish Who You Are: An officer is less likely to abuse a person, such as a star athlete, who is somewhat high profile. This is not to say you should abuse your status, but merely let them know that you are not some common hoodlum.

Limit Information: Don't start running off at the mouth; any information you give may be used against you. If the situation warrants it, don't talk until you have an attorney to advise you. The judicial system is like a game. Prosecutors for the most part could care less if you are guilty or innocent; they just want to win cases. Winning cases is how they advance their careers.

REMEMBER:

There are good and bad cops. You won't know which is which until you have a run-in with one.

Key Points to Remember:

- **Personality Conflicts** *are a part of life. Learn to work through them.*

- **Perceptions** *are more important than intentions.*

- **Diplomacy** *is the ability to successfully deal with others who oppose you.*

- **Coaches** *are human, and they make mistakes.*

- **BAAD Attitude** *will get you nowhere fast. Check Yourself Before You Wreck Yourself.*

- **Attitude Adjustments** *are a part of the game.*

Minor Adjustments

My sophomore year, it seemed like I was stuck at the fourth guard position for the longest. Finally, toward the middle of the season, I pulled Coach to side after practice. I asked him straight up: *"What do I have to do to play more? How can I improve my game? What are my weaknesses? What do you see as my strengths?"* His answers were simple and to the point. He told me I needed to work on my attitude in practice, man-to-man defense, and make better entry passes into the post. He said my strength was that I played smart basketball.

So I went out every day before, during and after practice, and worked on defensive drills and proper spacing for post entry passes. I also changed my attitude toward practicing. After about three weeks of this, I noticed that my game improved. Coach noticed as well, and I spent the rest of the year as the No. 2 guard. All I had to do was open my mouth, communicate, and make that slight attitude adjustment.

— S.T., Class of '94

Making Ends Meet, Without Jeopardizing Your Integrity

Everybody knows about Kareem Abdul-Jabbar, right? How the man who dazzled millions of fans with his hoop game ended up losing millions of the dollars he earned from the game. It's not that Kareem pissed away his money—not in the usual sense. He didn't smoke it up or gamble it away. Kareem lost his money the old-fashioned way: he trusted somebody else to handle it. Big mistake. That somebody, according to a 1992 *New York Times* article, was his agent. Kareem claimed that the agent mishandled $9 million in investments, which forced him to continue playing to earn it back.

At this point, you're a long way from having problems like Kareem. Still, there's no reason to put off understanding how to manage your money. Besides, pretty soon you won't have a choice. Once you make it to college, you'll have opportunities to screw up your finances. Even though your folks may still be in the picture, your name will start to appear on the bills, the checking account, the apartment lease.

This chapter will highlight ways to stretch the limited financial opportunities that are available to you without putting you at risk of being locked up or deemed ineligible. Specifically, we will talk about scholarships, financial aid, budgeting, investing, and responsibility.

> If you can't count, they can cheat you. If you can't read, they can beat you.
>
> —Toni Morrison

No Free Rides

It is a well-established fact that the NCAA and its member institutions, under the guise of amateurism, will not allow students-athletes financial rewards above and beyond what is deemed absolutely necessary (i.e., room and board, tuition, books, mandatory fees). Lets face it, if you do not come from a family who can afford to send you money, things may get a little tight. Statistics show that about fifty percent of all recruited student-athletes come from families who are basically broke. We realize that when cash flow is short, some people are tempted to use any means necessary to get paid. We want to discourage you from doing things that may jeopardize your athletic, academic, and professional future. Things such as credit card fraud, strong-arm robbery, unauthorized payments from agents or boosters may seem enticing under certain circumstances, but the consequences far outweigh any immediate benefits.

Vince's Rude Awakening

During my senior year of high school my counselor, Mrs. Sikes (not her real name) asked me if I had applied to the local junior college. Bewildered by her question I responded, "Lady, where have you been? I just signed a letter of intent for a full-ride scholarship to the University of Washington." *"There is no such thing as a full-ride scholarship,"* she said snobbishly, as if upset to discover that a Black youth could indeed win a scholarship to a prestigious university instead of being condemned to a junior college. "Vince, let's face it, you may have gotten A's and B's at this ghetto school, but at a prestigious school like the University of Washington, you'll probably get nothing more than C's and D's. Maybe you should consider junior college first."

While I despise the fact that she attempted to discourage me, I must admit that Mrs. Sikes did say one thing that I later discovered was true: *there are no full-ride scholarships.* There are only a series of one-year scholarships which are renewable on a yearly basis, depending upon the recommendation of the coach. Well, lady, this junior college material from the ghetto now has two degrees from the University of Washington, a professional certificate, and a graduate degree from the University of Michigan.

Scholarships, Financial Aid and Their Limitations

DIVISION I — FULL SCHOLARSHIPS

The majority of full ride (yearly renewal) scholarships are given by Division I (DI) schools, but not all DI schools offer athletic scholarships. As mentioned above, athletic scholarships are limited to tuition, food and housing, fees ,and books. With this type of aid comes many responsibilities on your part. In fact, the institution basically owns your ass for the duration of the time that you are receiving aid. So if you get out of line or don't pan out athletically, the school has the option to fire you (i.e., not renew). Rest assured that this does not happen very often, for any school that practiced such a policy on a regular basis would have a difficult time recruiting. While on scholarship at an NCAA member DI school, you are not allowed to work. However, you are allowed to receive a need-based Pell Grant if you and your family qualify financially. The Pell Grant, unlike a loan, does not have to be paid back. It is administered by the federal government.

DIVISION II — FULL-PARTIAL SCHOLARSHIPS

The scholarships given by schools in this division are not typically as comprehensive as those given by DI schools. Although some may offer full rides, they often provide only partial scholarships. A student receiving a partial scholarship will probably need to supplement his aid through grants and loans.

REMEMBER:
Division I athletics are a business. You are a part of the business and you are expected to contribute to the bottom line. Don't let anyone tell you otherwise.

DIVISION III — NO-SCHOLARSHIPS

Schools in this division, along with the Ivy League, (Harvard, Yale, Dartmouth, etc.) do not offer athletic scholarships. Any aid received at these institutions will have to be loans and grants. The aid packages offered by these schools and some DII schools can often be greater than that offered by DI schools. This is because your grants and loans may exceed the amount allowed by a full scholarship. Aid in this division is in no way contingent on your athletic performance; therefore, if you decide to quit the team, you can keep the cash as long as you continue going to school.

Note: See Chapter 3 for suggested reading on scholarship opportunities.

OTHER AID

There are numerous other forms of aid. They range from need and achievement-based scholarships to grants and loans supported by the federal government.

Administrative Expenses Gone, Now What?

OK, you've gotten some type of financial aid and the administrative essentials have been paid (i.e., tuition, fees, books, board). Let's hope you have received enough aid to feed your face as well. However, even on full-scholarship there isn't always enough money for you to eat adequately, particularly during the off-season. What this means is that you may have to do some creative money management if you hope to eat or do the various things that college students do (i.e., entertainment, driving, shopping).

In the following section, we will help you stretch the few dollars you are able to get your hands on. In planning this chapter, though, we had a difficult time coming up with viable suggestions. Why? Because somebody has obviously failed to realize that there's more to college expenses than tuition, food, room, and board. If you don't have money coming in from an outside source, most scholarships will not provide you much more than the necessities.

LIVING ON CAMPUS

Your first two years living on campus can be extremely difficult (many DI schools require scholarship athletes to live on campus during this period). Your housing is paid for and you get a weekly food stipend. Your main problem is a lack of cash, unless your folks are in a position to help. If they aren't, you will often walk around with little cash in your pockets. This can prove to be a psychologically and emotionally draining experience, because in college your social life may play as big a role in your experience as academics. How can you get props without loot? The solution to your cash problems may seem few and far between, but the following suggestions should help:

1. Establish a monthly budget to help control your spending and stick to it. (See section below on budgeting.)

2. Work a summer job and save as much as possible.

3. Ask relatives to send whatever they can spare. And if they have to sacrifice to send you money, then you had better show your appreciation by GRADUATING.

4. Apply for financial aid. Sometimes, in addition to your scholarship, you may also be eligible for other forms of financial assistance (i.e., Pell Grants, loans).

5. Try some of the shopping tips we suggest later in the chapter.

6. Get used to it. In two years your situation may improve. You may actually get to feel some cash pass through your hands each month.

Inevitably, every time we talk to young brothers on this subject, someone has to take the pimp-hustler attitude. Somebody will end up saying, "I'll just get a white chick with loot to take care of me." Listen, using *anyone* in this fashion is bad, so be a man and work out your own problems. Peace to you in trying to make ends meet—and try not to live larger than you can afford.

LIVING OFF CAMPUS

In your junior year at many DI schools, you may be allowed to live off campus and receive a scholarship check to pay your rent and utilities. While living off campus, it is important that you evaluate your monthly income (scholarship check) in relation to your monthly expenses (rent, utilities, food, gas, etc.).

Budgeting

We know that you may not currently qualify as a Wall Street Whiz Kid, but with a little common sense you can quickly learn to construct and stick to a budget. A budget can be defined as a financial game plan to manage your money. It does so by informing you of your cash status relative to your monthly financial obligations. You can follow the steps below to create a simple budget. We have also included a sample budget as a guideline for this process.

At the beginning of the month:

Step 1. Write down and add up all anticipated sources of cash for the month.
Step 2. Write down and add up all anticipated expenses for the month.
Step 3. Subtract the amount in Step 2 from the amount in Step 1. *Result:* Cash surplus or deficit.

If there's a surplus, you can choose to spend it by going to the movies, eating out or shopping, or

---

SAMPLE BUDGET

This budget is for someone with roommates, *something you should strongly consider.*

Income

Scholarship Check	$575
Summer Employment (contribution from savings)	75
Total Monthly Income	$650

Expenses

Rent	$350
Electricity/ Water	40
Gas/ Oil/ Coal (heating)	30
Phone	50
Groceries	75
Gasoline (auto)	40
Total Expenses	$585
Cash Surplus	$65

stash it away. If you're running a deficit, you should try to cut back. You may have to make some hard decisions, like getting rid of cable TV or eating out less. The trick is to exercise discipline and follow your budget, but don't make it so rigid that you will never be able to follow it.

As you can see, there isn't much left for savings in case of an emergency. It only takes one emergency to create a financial disaster and cause a setback for the rest of the year. This is why people should never live above their means. Yeah, we know that your means are already low, but it is the best you can do at the moment. Stick with us to learn how you can stretch your meager funds.

Expenditures

The following tips should assist you in spending your dollars wisely. We will only talk about expenses in this section because expenses are the flip side of income. When it comes to wise words about money, Ben Franklin supposedly said it best: "A penny saved is a penny earned."

General Shopping Rules

- Decisions to buy should be yours alone. Don't be influenced by others (i.e., salesmen, teammates). The item should fit some need and your budget.

- Time permitting, shop around for the best deals. Don't be shy about shopping at discount stores; they often carry name brands at substantially reduced prices.

- Shop for items during the time of year when they are cheapest. Seasonal items, such as winter gear, can be purchased cheaper in spring and summer.

- Avoid impulse buying.

- If you have an undying urge to shop, try to ease the urge by shopping at the ninety-nine cent store. Spending a little money may save you a lot.

Grocery Shopping

- Take a completed shopping list with you when you shop. Join a discount shopping club and buy in bulk. These clubs offer membership in exchange for a fee.

- Buy generic brands whenever possible. Generic brands typically have the exact ingredients as the name brands.

- Shop on a full stomach; it will keep you from buying food you can't afford.

Eating Out

- Markups at restaurants can be as high as 200 percent. Learn to cook and you can save lots of money on eating. Besides, women love men who can cook.

- Look for coupon books which offer two-for-one dining or percentage discounts. Don't be embarrassed to pull out a coupon; it is a mark of a wise and frugal man.

- When going out on dates, plan them for the daytime so you can take advantage of the lower lunch rates, which last until about 3 p.m.

- Explore different ethnic foods. Some of them may be cheaper than the traditional steak and potatoes. You might even find them enjoyable.

Food for Thought:

What type of fool prides himself on how much money he spends on an item? What he should be concerned with is how much he can save.

<u>Shopping for Gear</u>

- It is OK to dress like a bum in school. People expect as much.

- Discount department stores (Ross, TJ Maxx, Marshall's, etc.) often have name-brand items at considerable savings. If not, you can still save on underwear, socks, et cetera.

- Shop where you can negotiate the price (try to never pay the first price quoted). Even some larger department stores can and will negotiate prices. Ask to speak to the department manager. It also helps to take friends who want to buy similar items.

<u>Entertainment</u>

- **Movies:** Use discount coupons or go to matinees. Eat before you go or discretely bring your own food. Movie theaters often mark up food in excess of 200 percent.

- **Music:** Join compact disc clubs. The introductory offer often allows you to buy up to twelve discs for less than a dollar. The catch is that you have to buy a specified number of discs at regular price, but even with this the clubs are still a bargain. Wait a few weeks after a new release to purchase it; the price drops considerably.

- **Miscellaneous:** (Cheap thrills) means of entertainment can save you money as well as expand your cultural horizons.

  Museums. Start with those on campus, then explore others in the city.

  Historical landmarks. Call the visitors bureau for information on local attractions.

Picnics. Take the initiative and plan one for your favorite girl.

Flea markets. Here's an opportunity to buy something nice and inexpensive.

Scenic drives. Depending on the part of the country, your area may offer some very beautiful sites.

Volunteer work in your spare time. It can be fun.

Free activities: hiking/biking, arts festivals, food fairs, etc. These activities can be fun and healthy.

Travel

- Plan trips as far in advance as possible to assure the lowest fare.

- Credit card companies often offer student flight vouchers and discounts. Ask about them.

- Look for two-for-one deals offered by airlines. Ask your travel agent for details.

Phone Bills

- Write letters instead of making that expensive long distance call. This will also help to improve your writing skills, and your girl will love reading them.

- Call during the early morning or late evening when long distance rates are lower.

- When you call long distance, ask the other party to call you back. Explain that you are a poor starving student; the other party should understand.

- Avoid unnecessary phone service features (i.e., caller ID, three-way calling). These features may appear cheap, but they quickly add up.

- If you have roommates and share the phone, make sure they are personally accountable for their own calls. (Don't volunteer to have the bill in your name.)

- Shop around for the best long distance rates.

Utilities

- If you have roommates, make sure everyone understands the need to conserve. Everybody should be conscientious about turning off lights, appliances, et cetera.

- Purchase an inexpensive window insulation kit to reduce heat loss from your home.

- If you can't afford the kit, athletic tape can be used to seal windows sills.

- During the winter, wear more clothing indoors and turn down the heat.

- Take shorter showers, and don't let water run unnecessarily while washing dishes.

FINANCIAL PRINCIPLES

By now, you should be aware of the fact that excess money may be limited. This does not mean that you should skip learning the basic principles of finance. Whether you make it to a league, work in corporate America, or start a business, it will be imperative that you have a basic understanding of how to manage your finances. Whatever amount you earn, it should be your decision as to how it's spent. You should never allow others to handle your money without first understanding what they are going to do with it. It doesn't matter if the person has Ph.D, CPA, CFA, Esq., LLM or any other designation behind their name. If they can't explain how they will handle your money in a way that you can understand, *fire them*. Better yet, make sure you fully understand the most basic financial principles, defined below, *before* hiring someone to follow them for you.

10 Basic Financial Principles

1. **Annuity.** A specified income payable at stated intervals for a fixed or a contingent period. Lay terms: The lottery is an excellent example of an annuity. Upon winning, the recipient is paid a certain amount of money per year for a certain number of years.

2. **Assets.** A single item of ownership having exchange value. Lay terms: Something that belongs to you that has financial or personal value (money, education, etc.).

3. **Tax Shelter.** A method used by taxpayers to legally avoid or reduce tax liabilities. Lay terms: This is a way to pay less income tax, thereby keeping more of your hard-earned loot in your pocket. Find a knowledgeable financial adviser to establish a tax shelter, because illegal shelters can cause major financial problems.

4. **Commodity.** An article of large-scale trade such as butter, coffee, sugar, or grains. Lay terms: An item so similar to another item that if you exchange them you can hardly tell the difference. Many student-athletes are considered commodities in that if you get injured you can be substituted with little difference in the quality of play.

5. **Present Value.** The estimated current worth of money to be received (or paid). Lay terms: How much is a dollar received five years from now worth today? The answer should be less than a dollar because you won't be able to buy as much. This concept is often used in professional sports contract negotiations. The contract amount on paper may say $20 million, but the actual values will be less because the money is paid over a period of time. If you ever sign a phat contract make sure you know the true value because someone with a seemingly smaller contract may actually be getting more.

(continued on next page)

6. **Inflation.** A substantial rise in prices caused by an undue expansion in paper money or bank credit. Lay terms: As people get more money they tend to buy more. As they buy more, those selling products or services demand higher prices.

7. **Interest.** A sum paid or charged for the use of money or for borrowing money. Lay terms: If you loan someone five dollars and they aren't an exceptionally good friend you may want seven back; the extra two dollars represents interest.

8. **Investment.** Devoting, using, or giving money, time, talent, et cetera, and receive something more in return. Lay terms: You have just acquired a little cash. You can buy a house which may be worth more next year or you can buy a 560 Benz which you know will be worth less. Which one is an investment?

9. **Liabilities.** Obligations resulting from past transactions that require the payment of money and/or the provision of goods or services. Lay terms: When you borrow five dollars from a not-so-good friend, you have a liability until you pay it back.

10. **Stocks and bonds.** Stocks are shares of a corporation. Bonds are interest-bearing loans made to a corporation or government. Lay terms: Your boy needs money to start a business. If you give it to him with the understanding that if the business fails he doesn't owe you anything (i.e., you share the risk), this is similar to having stock in a company. When the company loses, you lose, too. On the other hand if the business fails and you still expect to be paid back, this is similar to a bond (loan) to a company.

ESTABLISHING BANKING RELATIONSHIPS

For many of you, college will be your first opportunity to open a savings and/or checking account. Hopefully, this will be the start of many new banking relationships as you continue to be educated about how to become a productive and prosperous tax-paying citizen. Here's how you can develop these relationships:

- Choose a bank that values your business, whether you're depositing $1 million or $100. Make sure that the employees are friendly, respectful, and helpful.

- Shop around for the bank offering the best interest rates and charging the lowest fees. Don't worry, all deposits up to $100,000 are insured by the U.S. government's Federal Deposit Insurance Corporation (FDIC).

- Take into consideration whether the bank can help you begin establishing credit by offering you a student credit card. (See Establishing Credit.)

- Use your bank to help you begin to understand more about financial principles. Don't be shy; ask your representative about mutual funds, stocks, bonds, et cetera.

- Learn to balance your checkbook and keep it balanced. Don't forget to keep track of your trips to the ATM.

ESTABLISHING AND MAINTAINING CREDIT

Before Naughty By Nature made famous the acronym OPP, there was a famous financial acronym, OPM. OPM (Other People's Money) is the basic principle surrounding financial credit and is a lot safer than OPP. As a future businessperson, you will need to learn how to use OPM to your advantage.

The funny thing about credit is that people will offer it even when you don't have the funds to repay it. Department stores, banks, auto dealers, etc. will offer college students credit based on their anticipated earnings or based on their parents' (i.e., cosigners') ability to pay. In fact, some banks refer to these arrangements as "Kiddie Credit"; if you don't pay, they simply hound your parents.

Overzealous creditors provide a tremendous opportunity to establish a personal credit history (track record of the timely payment of bills). A good credit history will be needed when you buy homes, automobiles, electronic equipment, et cetera. Your credit history will follow you around for life, so don't mess it up. When you apply for credit, the creditor will input your Social Security number into a credit bureau computer that will show your credit history. If you don't pay your bills on time, it will appear on your credit report. Once you screw up, it may take years to reestablish a good credit history.

Also remember that your rental history and utilities go on your credit report as well. A former student-athlete told us of a roommate who ran up the phone bill so high that it was shut off. This student informed the phone company that it was his room-mate's fault, and refused to pay. However, some three years later when he was attempting to purchase his first home, the unpaid phone bill appeared on his credit report. After considerable delay, he eventually cleared up the problem. So don't think you are getting over by not paying your bills. That could backfire.

Credit Tips

- Discipline is key; don't take on more credit than you can handle.
- With credit, the longer you take to pay it back, the more it costs.
- Apply for credit cards that do not charge a membership fee.
- Shop around for credit cards which have the lowest possible interest rates.
- Since you must have something to pay to have a credit history, use your cards wisely. Use only when necessary and pay the full debt the following month.

Giving Something Back

The need has never been greater: once you manage to get yours, give some of it back.

More than ever, African-Americans need to spend their dollars in their own communities. It used to be easy to identify the physical African-American community, especially business districts such as Atlanta's Auburn Avenue ("Sweet Auburn"), home of Atlanta Life Insurance Company and other Black-owned businesses. Now, the African-American community and its business districts aren't quite so easy to identify. But just because it's harder for us to find each other, it's still worth the search.

The need to give back, to do business with qualified Black accountants, doctors, attorneys, and other businesspeople, still exists. Lord knows, the last thing anybody else in this country is concerned about is acting in *our* best interest. Members of other ethnic groups support their communities with real dollars; for the sake of

REMEMBER:
Don't let easily obtained credit cause you to lose sight of your financial objectives.

empowerment and survival, we must do the same thing.

But it's not all about money exchanging hands for goods or services. Giving back means investing in people, especially our young people. It means that the young brother who's talented—and lucky—enough to make it to the pros should skip the donation to his university's scholarship program. His money belongs first in the 'hood where he grew up. Those dollars can help a school system that is so broke it can't even afford to have an athletic program. Anybody who can't understand that has a problem.

African-American student-athletes must realize how instrumental you can be in educating America and effecting change during your career. The opportunity earned to embark on an athletic career usually overshadows the opportunity to be educated and demonstrate to youths that financial success can be achieved through many career paths. More importantly, you have the opportunity to gain some basic business skills that can be utilized after your athletic career. Money is the only universal language, and it is very unfortunate that few professional African-American athletes utilize their wealth, contacts and influence to begin successful businesses which appeal to the mass market and then circulate the revenues in the African-American community to spawn additional business. Finally, athletes must educate themselves about the many African-American attorneys, accountants, and media representatives fully capable of providing outstanding services and exploit their skills.

—D. N., Class of 1996

Not What You Know, But Who You Know

As a student-athlete, you will have the opportunity to meet and socialize with some of the most affluent and powerful people in the country. This chapter will guide you on how to maximize your opportunities. Remember, the greatest opportunities in the world are meaningless unless they are acted upon and turned into something positive.

So, What Is Networking?

Here's how we define it: *Networking is the process of meeting as many positive people as possible in order to make the world smaller and your opportunities greater.* Networking is an exponential process during which you meet one person and that person puts you in touch with two other people. Those two people hook you up with four other people, and so on. Experts in the fields of communications and demography say that the average person knows at least 300 other people. That means we are only four to six people away from knowing everyone on the planet. Now, that is a powerful thought!

Testing Your Networking Skills

The brief quiz that follows will give you a quick way of assessing your current networking skills. Some of you already have tremendous skills in this area, but there is always room for improvement. Our goal is to get you to make networking a

No person is your friend (or kin) who demands your silence, or denies your right to grow and be perceived as fully blossomed as you were intended.

—Alice Walker

daily part of your life and to capitalize on the enormous opportunities your status as a student-athlete affords you.

The good thing about this quiz is that you get to score it yourself. To determine your score answer each question using a scale of 1 to 3 (1 = never, 2 = sometimes, 3 = always) in terms of how you currently act on a daily basis. Answer the questions truthfully so you can arrive at a realistic starting point for improving your skills. When you finish the test, total your score to determine where you fall in the range from Freshman to All-American.

NETWORKING SKILLS QUIZ   Scale of 1 to 3 *(1 = never, 2 = sometimes, 3 = always)*

1. I make it a habit to make others feel comfortable. I don't pride myself on looking "hard" and angry, even though I may have cause to be that way. ☐

2. I convey an attitude of confidence and professionalism. ☐

3. People who know me have a high opinion of me and aren't afraid to recommend me to others. ☐

4. I understand the opportunities and responsibilities that come with my status, but I don't abuse the privileges. ☐

5. I make it a habit to meet as many people as possible. ☐

6. I am a gracious, courteous and likable person, and people can sense my sincerity. ☐

7. I try to keep my commitments in a timely and professional fashion. ☐

8. I meet people and think about how they can help me and/or someone else I know, as well as how I might be able to help them. ☐

9. I never make value judgments of a person based on superficial characteristics such as status, occupation, financial wealth, et cetera. ☐

10. I am not afraid to ask people for their assistance or to offer assistance. ☐

11. I devise strategies to meet people I need and/or want to meet regardless of their status or profession. ☐

Test Continued

12. I actively work to develop my network by making calls, writing letters, sending thank-you notes, inviting people to lunch, etc. ☐

13. I call people when they give me their number and ask me to call them, and also when they don't. ☐

14. I regularly and systematically keep in touch with those who are currently a part of my network. ☐

15. I make an outline of what I want to say and accomplish before making a networking call. ☐

16. I mentally prepare for networking activities in order to get the maximum benefits. ☐

17. I actively work to keep up with current events by reading and watching the news, so that I will have plenty to talk about when I meet people. ☐

18. I am involved in other beneficial activities outside of playing sports. ☐

19. I enjoy helping others, even when there in no immediate personal benefit to me. ☐

20. When I meet people, I make a serious attempt to remember their names. ☐

21. I try very hard not to burn bridges. ☐

22. I am someone others know they can rely on. ☐

23. I make sure that my friends also understand the importance of networking. ☐

24. When meeting people, I show an interest in them. ☐

25. I realize that I am a most-wonderful person and why wouldn't people want to get to know me? ☐

TOTAL

TOTAL	Quiz Key
70 - 75	All-American
62 - 69	Backup
46 - 61	Benchwarmer
25 - 45	Freshman

Strategic Networking

Hopefully, you did OK on the quiz. If you didn't, this chapter should assist you in the Art of Strategic Networking. Through this process, you develop *thoughts* and *actions* that result in your meeting positive people. Strategic networking can be developed if you apply some of the following concepts to your life. Even if you scored as an All-American, there are always things you can learn to become All-World. Check this section for new techniques or insights.

NETWORKING MENTALITY

Once you develop a networking mentality, meeting and developing relationships will become second nature. A networking mentality comes from recognizing opportunities to meet people and quickly evaluating how those meetings can be mutually beneficial. The operative word here is "mutually." Nothing turns people off faster than meeting other people who are out to take as much as they can get without giving something in return. When networking, be prepared to give something of yourself in the process. And don't forget that meeting new people is a natural activity, one that allows you to express a sincere curiosity about others as well as have some fun.

Picture this: you're on a plane and a distinguished, well-dressed gentleman sits next to you. You say hello, he responds and then begins reading a magazine. No doubt you're thinking, "I wonder what this guy does for a living? I should ask, but he is really into that magazine ... I know, I'll wait until they serve snacks, then he will have to put the magazine down." When the snack arrives, you say: "That sure is a nice suit you're wearing. I need to be in your profession. By the way, what business are you in?" The gentleman tells you he's the chief

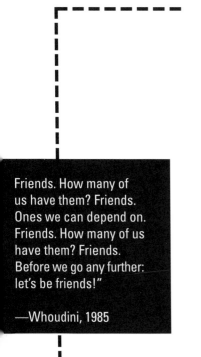

"Friends. How many of us have them? Friends. Ones we can depend on. Friends. How many of us have them? Friends. Before we go any further: let's be friends!"

—Whoudini, 1985

financial officer of XYZ Corp, the largest maker of widgets in the world. You start thinking about your boy who is looking for a job in the widget business and you tell the gentleman about him. Before you know it, you have the guy's business card and you've passed on your boy's name. Two weeks later, your boy has a job and XYZ Corp. has a qualified new employee. Way to look out!

Attitude Adjustment

One day my position coach called me and some of my dawgs into his office to discuss our behavior in the dorms. Coach made the comment, "I'm getting complaints from the dorms that you guys are running around intimidating people because you guys look so mean. Stop walking around looking so mean. You guys scare people when you do that." At the time he said it I was offended. I thought, how dare this man tell us to stop looking mean. Shit, I look mean because I'm mad. I'm a Black man living in White America; how else should I be? In retrospect, I realize that all white folks weren't out to get me and that all Black folks weren't out to help me. I probably could have done a lot more networking, had I not intimidated so many people. I wonder how many potentially valuable relationships I missed out on as a result of my attitude.

—K. B., Class of 1989

DEVELOPING THE RIGHT ATTITUDE

Your attitude and the way you present yourself socially will affect how people perceive you. Being "hard" probably is not the best way to develop a network of friends and contacts. Sometimes when we approached young brothers while writing this book, they acted as though they wanted to beat us down. This type of first impression might be effective and appropriate on a late night in an alley, but it doesn't work well when networking. The reality, though, is that tough guys do very little networking because they often alienate the people they need to interact with.

The coach in the above story was right for checking the young brothers, although maybe not for all the right reasons. In our discussions with K. B., the coach appeared to be more concerned with the well-being of the other students. It would have been more effective had the coach emphasized to the young men that they were actually sabotaging their own progress by being anti-social. Although the other students' fear may have been in part the results of stereotyping and ignorance, the reality is that this fear *(real or imagined)* does exist. Therefore, you must do your part to develop techniques to make others feel more comfortable. A good starting point is the simplest international gesture of friendliness known to mankind, a *smile*. Save the angry looks for game day or for those late nights when you are walking home alone from the library. This is not to say that you should shuffle along with a big dumb grin on your face. Quite the contrary. In this art of networking, your job is to influence the perception others have of you. You can still maintain a sense of dignity and pride, but do so in a manner which does not limit your ability to develop relationships.

FRIENDS AND NETWORKING

A friend, as defined by Webster's, is *"a valued associate or acquaintance."* The key term here is "valued." Ask yourself what you value about your current friends. If you can't come up with an answer, maybe these people are acquaintances, not friends.

Fact is, valued associates are difficult to come by. So when the opportunity to develop one presents itself, take full advantage of it. Seek individuals whose goals and aspirations parallel your own. Surrounding yourself with real friends will make networking easier. Together, you can attend functions with the clear intentions of meeting as many people as possible and not worry that your agendas will clash.

DEVELOP KNOWLEDGE

A wide base of knowledge will make it easier for you to interact with people, particularly if their interests differ from yours. Have you ever been involved in a group discussion and the subject changes to something like German politics or global warming? After that, you probably felt out of place. Had you known just a little about the subject, you could have possibly avoided this feeling, as well as added to the conversation. We cannot overemphasize the importance of being a well-rounded brother. The way to become well rounded is to read, study, and listen. At the very least, you should skim the newspaper on a daily basis—and we don't mean only the sports section.

Maximizing Sports-Related Interactions

As mentioned earlier, college athletics can be a gateway to success both inside and outside the athletic arena. Most people love associating with athletes; in fact our entire country seems to have a love affair with sports. More important, power brokers (businessmen, politicians, etc.) often have a passion for sports, particularly college sports. This is obvious, given the millions of dollars donated to athletic departments by alumni.

WHAT DOES ALL THIS MEAN TO YOU?

First, there may never be a better opportunity to interact and establish relationships with people in positions of power. These relationships will, for the most part, be due to your athletic status. It is imperative that you take full advantage of these opportunities because they may disappear after your athletic career ends. Many of these people will not offer you the same amount of attention after your playing days since new kids will come along and take your place. But, if you maintain communications, these relationships can extend beyond your playing days. Here's how Andre developed and maintained a mutually beneficial relationship.

Andre and Jim: A Special Relationship

After graduating in 1987, I contacted Jim Kenyon at his office where I had worked during the summers. I asked about a job in the real estate development firm of which he was president. Jim told me to come and see him when I got to Los Angeles. When I arrived, no jobs were available. Instead, Jim asked me if I was still into auto detailing, then offered me the opportunity to open a detailing shop on the ground floor of his building. He also offered to loan me the start-up cost. I took advantage of the opportunity. After two years of hard work and dedication, I built the business into a fairly profitable enterprise. I was then offered an opportunity to open a second location, so I went back to Jim with a proposal to finance my second location, and he agreed. This was all possible due to our longtime mentor/mentee relationship. I had always shown myself to be a hardworking and dependable person. I asked Jim lots of questions and sought as much knowledge from him as possible. Jim Kenyon helped change my life. His willingness to assist me and others makes him a role model for all philanthropists.

The above story illustrates the importance of maintaining postgraduate relationships. Jim Kenyon provided direction, financial support, and solid advice for a young man who was in dire need of all three. Student-athletes need to build more solid relationships along these lines: relationships that will endure over time.

FOLLOW THESE TIPS FOR MAXIMIZING YOUR INTERACTIONS:

Avoid being pigeon-holed. Even though athletics may be the only topic people want to discuss with you, make it a point to talk about what's happening in business, politics, international affairs, et cetera. You don't have to be an expert; general knowledge will do the trick. You can obtain this by reading and watching the TV news.

Show confidence. Even though you may be interacting with some of the most influential people in the country, you should avoid being starstruck. Many of these people will be in as much awe of your accomplishments as you will be of theirs. Greet people with a firm handshake while stating your name clearly and confidently.

Put others in the spotlight. During your interactions, the conversation will usually focus on you or your team. Here's another opportunity to impress people by showing interest in them. Make others the center of attention by asking questions. You will quickly find that people love to talk about themselves. Don't know where to start? Pick questions from the list below.

- How did you get to your current position within your company?
- What other types of jobs have you held?
- What was your major in school? Why did you choose it?
- What type of preparation do you suggest I make in order to secure a job in your field?
- What do you see as the major problems affecting your business?
- How important do you think a graduate degree is in the current job market?
- If you had it to do all over again, would you change anything about your career?
- Who are the major competitors in your business?
- Are their any summer internship opportunities where I can really learn something?
- Do you have a card so I can contact you at some later date?

Seize every opportunity. All of your networking opportunities may not be in a formal setting. Many of them will occur in the locker room after a game, when you are butt-naked! Still, you must not miss out on these chances. No joke: when you meet people under these circumstances, follow the same principals you would in a more formal setting. Although you may be tired or upset from losing, try to be gracious.

Develop the relationship. You've made an initial impression, but your work is not done. You still need to develop the meeting into a lasting relationship. The key is to take the initiative. There are very few businesspeople, especially alumni, who won't be flattered by your interest. Here's how to further cultivate your relationship.

- Shortly after your initial meeting, follow up with a note or phone call expressing how much you enjoyed meeting the person.

- If you meet someone you especially like, ask the person to consider being your mentor.

- Call your contacts and ask for the best time to tour their place of business or discuss future career opportunities.

- Every week, call at least one contact you haven't spoken to in the last month.

- Find out where the person works and pay an unannounced visit. This wouldn't fly if you were already in the work force, but it's acceptable for a young person. Depending on the adult, this kind of behavior is considered (a) gutsy or (b) cute. Besides, you're not the only one who benefits. The adult who takes time out of his busy day to share his knowledge with a kid who's not his own will score major brownie points with his boss and colleagues.

Don't be afraid to ask for help. One of the problems that comes from being a member of a proud and gifted people is that we are often too *proud to beg*. Just kidding! Seriously, if there is something you need from someone, simply ask. The worst thing that could happen is not that the answer is no, but that you missed an opportunity for help by not asking.

NOTE: When dealing with alumni and/or others related to the athletic program, make sure that you understand the NCAA regulations governing these relationships. We called the NCAA to find out the rules, but we received extremely vague information. So, explain to your coaches that your intent is only to develop relationships for your future. They should be able to understand this and give guidance.

Tapping into Others on or Around Campus

In addition to the many powerful and influential people you will meet, you will also be surrounded by everyday folks. Although they may not currently possess the same power as some of the captains of industry, they can still be a tremendous resource for networking. You should never discount a person based on any superficial basis such as status, appearance, race, or other irrelevant characteristic.

As a student-athlete, you'll get accustomed to people taking the initiative to approach you. Still, you should not let others do all the work. Remember, your goal is to meet as many positive people as possible. To do so, you will have to confront some issues that have long been associated with the college athlete, issues such as the perception of arrogance and intimidation on the part of jocks. Then there's the fear many people have of big Black men. And like it or not, you'll have to deal with good, old-fashioned jealousy—you've got the talent and the status that others may never have.

The Company You Keep

When I was in school, my teammates used to dawg me because they often saw me walking around campus with people they considered square or nerdy. What do you expect: I was a premed major and of course most of my classmates didn't look like the majority of my teammates. I didn't let the teasing get to me and I continued to study and hang out with my premed classmates. The funny thing is that I often enjoyed the company of these so-called square people. Seven years later I rarely talk to my old teammates, but my premed boys, we talk all the time. We have even done business together.

—Dr. R. P., Class of 1988

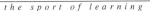

Make an effort to break down the barriers that for too long have prevented student-athletes from being a part of mainstream college life. Take under your wing the frail, nerdy kid who would love to be a part of your crew. Extend your hand to the weird girl down the hall who seems to have no friends. Say a few kind words to the short, dumpy security guard. These actions won't kill you, and you may make a true friend in the process.

Community-Based Networking

America has an abundance of youths who lack leadership and direction. To help them, African-Americans have set up a number of successful support systems through churches, clubs, schools, and other organizations. Still, there's a need for successful, young African-Americans to return to the community and bond with these kids. Every young brother reading this book is capable of helping to fill this void. By becoming involved, you will also have the opportunity to meet politicians, other public servants, and community leaders. Such an opportunity could be a valuable tool in building your network.

It is unfortunate that community service is not a mandatory part of every college athletic program. Even worse, it's a sad commentary on our society that performing community service is required usually only as punishment for committing a crime (i.e., moving violations, misdemeanors, etc.). Community service should be encouraged, if not mandated, by all college coaches.

Whether you use it in a community-based setting, on campus, or in an off-campus social setting, networking is a tool that can have a profound impact on your present situation and your future career. All it takes to reap the benefits are practice, initiative, and a little common sense.

CHAPTER 11. FEMALES

The College Coed and You

It's All Good

"Your crib or mine?" "Mine," she said. "My girl is away for the weekend and we will have the place all to ourselves." When we left the party, she put her arm around my waist and let her hand fall down to squeeze my ass, as if she couldn't wait to get her freak on.

Her dorm room was on the other side of campus and we stepped with the quickness. Neither one of us could wait to get there. When we finally got there, she put on Jodeci and lit some incense to get the mood straight. By this time, my junk was hard as a rock. Damn, I couldn't wait to hit that chumpy. I was gonna break her off somethin.'

"You're so fine," she said with her thick pretty lips. The girl started tonguing me, stuck her tongue all down my throat. She rubbed my junk and felt how hard I was. Dawg, I was ready to throw my junk.

"Let's do it, baby," I said. And damned if she didn't pull her skirt right off of her fat ass. I put my hand between her thighs and by the feel of it I knew she was good to go. She even let me pull her panties off. Then just as I was about to hit it, she said, "NO, NO, NO. I don't want to do this. Not tonight."

—M. T. C., Class of 1996

> Boys Make Babies—
> Men Take Care of Them.
>
> —Dr. Jawanza Kunjufu

Question: Can she do that and get away with it?

Answer: Yes, she can. And if you forcefully take what isn't yours, you could be tried and convicted as a rapist. In the eyes of the law, the above situation is no different from some stranger grabbing a women in a dark alley and forcing himself upon her.

Let us first *apologize* to anyone who may be offended by this graphic illustration, but we feel it necessary to emphasize that when it comes to another person's body, *no means no.*

The college campus provides many opportunities to interact with females, and through these interactions come many potential pitfalls. The issues covered in this chapter are those which we feel have the greatest potential for preventing you from achieving your goals. And, no we will not cover *how to get your mack on.* We will start our discussion with the earlier example of potential date rape.

Date Rape

> *date-rape:* **1.** forced, manipulated, or coerced sexual acts by a friend or acquaintance occurring in a date-like situation; **2.** forcing sexual acts after a person has said no; **3.** participating in sexual acts with a person who is not 100% consenting; **4.** sex act with someone who is permanently or temporally mentally or physically impaired.

The first definition is the most commonly used definition of date rape. This issue is one of the biggest that students now face. As for the last three definitions, you will probably never go wrong if you incorporate them into your personal definition of date rape.

WARNING: No Safe Sex.
We would be remiss if we did not say that the only truly safe sex is no sex. However, we are not going to tell you how to live your life, but we will try to inform you of the dangers of engaging in sexual relations outside of a loving monogamous relationship.

Date rape is very controversial in that it is difficult to ascertain who is telling the truth. If a disgusting, low-life male did force himself upon a woman, he more than likely would not tell the truth. When it comes to being accused of rape, two things are certain. If you are convicted of such a heinous crime, your career and your life will never be the same. The same is true for the victim.

Let's analyze the previously mentioned scenario. In the above illustration, many men would label the young lady a tease. They would not consider her words as a real indication that she didn't want to engage in sex. We personally would consider this young lady guilty of bad judgment, having let the situation escalate as it did. However, you must remember that even young ladies with bad judgment have the right at any point to say no.

Avoiding situations where you could be accused of rape has even greater significance for you, the high-profile campus celebrity. Being an athlete can have many blessings. One of them is more accessibility to females. Yes, there will be shallow people who will jock you solely because of your athletic prowess. That means you have more of a burden to scrutinize the situation and be aware of the added responsibility on your part. As a high-profile individual, your actions will be viewed under a microscope by fans, faculty, media, etc. For this reason, you must always be aware of your actions and assume that someone is watching your every move. Ask yourself this: *"Would I be doing this if my mother was watching me?"* Or try this one: *"Would I appreciate a man doing this to my sister?"* If the answer to either question is no, you probably ought to think twice before doing it.

Ask yourself this:

"Would I be doing this if my mother was watching me?" Or try this one: *"Would I appreciate a man doing this to my sister?"* If the answer to either question is no, you probably ought to think twice before doing it.

Mike Tyson: Former heavyweight champion "Iron" Mike Tyson is a classic example of a high-profile individual convicted of date rape. Now, if the heavyweight champion of the world can be convicted of date rape, what do you think could happen to you? Absolutely no one is above the law, nor should they be.

So, you're probably wondering how to avoid such a situation. Well, you will have the greatest chance of avoiding this stigmatizing and life-altering event by using *good judgment*. Here's what else you need to know:

1. No Means No

We men think there are times when a woman says, "No!" or "Stop!" or "We shouldn't do this!" without meaning it. We suspect what she really means is, "I don't want you to think I'm easy," or "I will do it, but I want you to still respect me." On the other hand, we could be mistaken. See how much room there is for misinterpretation? The best way to avoid this potentially costly mistake is to always assume that *no means no*. If you are unsure, try saying something like this: "I really respect you, but I don't know if you really mean no. Tell me if that is what you really mean." Communication is the key. Still, the best thing to remember is that *no means no*.

2. Show Respect

Always show respect for women, even when you think they don't deserve it. When people are humiliated they can become vindictive. Say you're involved with a women who is out there bad. She's a pretty girl and, despite her reputation, seems to be a nice person. You start dating her on a regular basis, and she tells you that she has changed her ways. In other words, she only wants to be with you. You believe her, but soon find out that she is still up to her old habits. At this point, you are pissed and hurt, so when you see her in the crowded student union, you con-template calling her the "B-word," "S-word," "H-word," and every other derogatory word you can think of. However, you're an enlightened young brother who knows that you should always respect women. Besides, you knew the woman's past from the start. Therefore, you may want to be more selective in your involvement with people.

3. Avoid the Temporarily Mentally Impaired
This situation is consistent with the fourth definition of date rape that we mentioned earlier. Avoid women who have this problem; you never know how this type of person will react the next morning. People who are temporarily impaired, we're talking about those who are drunk or high, can lead to trouble.

4. Skip Orgies and Multiple Sex Partners
If you end up in some precarious situation with two or more people who are prepared to engage in sexual intercourse, run! What you thought appeared to be consensual sex at night may be considered gang rape in the morning. A few moments of sexual pleasure is not worth it.

5. Stop the Violence Before It Starts
If you find yourself in a volatile situation (i.e., you're getting upset), the best advice we can offer is to simply walk away. This can save you from doing something you will regret later. As Dr. T. Garrott Benjamin says, "Real men never lift a hand to women unless they are reaching to Heaven to bless her."

Violence towards women of any kind is unacceptable and includes more than just rape or physical abuse. The following definition is derived from material formulated by the Northeastern University Mentors in Violence Prevention (MVP) Project:

GENDER VIOLENCE: A Definition

Rape/ Date Rape	or	Battering/ Abuse	or	Sexual Harassment	=	VIOLENCE AGAINST WOMEN !
Forcing sex on another person		Hitting, beating, pushing & shoving		Unwanted sexual advances		
Forced manipulated or coerced sexual acts, occurring in a date like situation		Verbally abusing your partner		Verbal sexual innuendoes and suggestions		
Forcing sexual acts after your partner says "no"		Property destruction, vandalism and actions causing financial hardship		Vulgar sexual jokes & references to women as sexual objects		
Forced oral sex or sodomy of any kind		Creating an element of fear and intimidation in the relationship		Spreading degrading and humiliating sexual rumors about your partner		

SO WHAT CAN BE DONE TO PREVENT VIOLENCE AGAINST WOMEN?

The MVP Project suggests a few things you can do. Although the list is not exhaustive, it along with good moral values will go along way in preventing abuse, not only against women, but against all human beings.

Things Men can do to Prevent Violence Against Women

- Understand how your own attitudes and actions perpetuate sexism and violence, and work toward changing them.

- Confront sexist, racist, homophobic, and all other bigoted remarks or jokes.

- Don't fund sexism. Don't purchase any magazine, rent any video, see any film, or purchase any music that portrays women in a sexually degrading or violent manner.

- If you know of any woman who is being abused, cautiously ask her if you can help. If you have a friend or teammate who is abusing his girlfriend or other women, talk to him and encourage him to get assistance. Actively get involved if you see someone in need of assistance (i.e., call police, bring attention to attacker, etc.).

- Read about yourself. Read articles, essays, books about masculinity, gender inequality, and the root causes of sexual violence. Educate yourself and others about the connections between larger social forces and the conflicts between individual women and men.

- Take courses on gender-related topics in sociology, history, psychology, etc.

Additional Resources:

National Council on Child Abuse & Family Violence
1155 Connecticut Avenue Suite 300
Washington, D.C. 20036
(800) 222-2000

Mentors in Violence Prevention Project
Center for the Study of Sport in Society - Northeastern University
360 Huntington Avenue Suite 16 CP
Boston, MA 02115
(617) 373-4025

The National Resource Center on Domestic Violence
(800) 537-2238

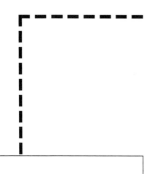

REMEMBER:
Art often imitates life. No matter how big a star you become, there are still those in society who will still see you only as a Star Negro.

- Organize, join, or support a group of peers in school to work against sexism and violence. Participate and encourage dialogue and awareness in group discussions.

If you are involved in any type of violence against women, brother, *please, please,* seek professional help!

Ain't no Bitches in Here

Some of us have literally lost our minds. We think nothing about disrespecting our African sisters by calling them *"bitches"* and *"ho's."* Sure, there are women out there living bad, but we should work toward not passing judgment on our sisters. Somehow, our women have survived centuries of brutality at the hands of men, from being prostituted and raped by slave owners to being assaulted and molested by fathers and uncles. Through it all, they have continued to nourish, comfort, and support the Black race. Obviously, our sisters deserve not to be equated with female dogs and prostitutes.

Sex and Race

For many of you, college will be your first real experience dealing with women of different races, particularly white women. Interracial dating is a controversial issue because even though it is tolerated in our society, it is still not totally accepted. *It will not be totally accepted until all of us recognize that we all come from the same race: the human race.* Andrew Hacker, in his best-selling book *Two Nations*, notes that—even today—if African-American men are caught assaulting white women, they will be more severely punished by the law. Even "liberal" Hollywood has not embraced the idea of Black men being intimately involved with white women. For example, during the early test screening of the movie *Drop Zone,* starring Wesley Snipes, Snipes kissed his white female sidekick (Yancy Butler). Audiences hated this so much that the kiss was dropped in the final version.

Pregnancy, Fathering, and Responsibility

Now, we know some brothers don't see a problem with knocking up women. In fact, for these fellas, the more women they can impregnate, the better. It's a fertility trip, having your seed planted all over the yard. This type of behavior is totally irresponsible and detrimental to the creation of loving and productive children. Men who indulge in such behavior obviously have a problem with low self-esteem, since the only way they can build themselves up is by bringing down women and children. To those fellas, we say: our days of "breeding" are over. That's something we were once forced to do. Today, we are free to make babies out of love for our partners and a planned desire to have children. Making babies for any other reason is bogus.

Got 'Em

A conversation between roommates during their sophomore year of college (the names have been changed).

Shannon: "Girl, I've been thinking about a way to secure my future with Brian. You know he's going pro in two years."
Dawn: "Oh yeah . . . and what way is this?"
Shannon: "I'm going to have his baby. I refuse to let some other ho' get my man. He's goin' pro and I'm gonna be there. If I have his baby, he'll have to marry me."
Dawn: "He doesn't have to do anything."
Shannon: "Oh, he will. And besides, at the very least I can get that child support."
Dawn: "He knows you're on the Pill . . . how are you going to explain it?"
Shannon: "There's always that one percent chance and I'm going to be it."

Result: Shannon succeeded. A baby was born and Brian did marry her, but Brian was not drafted. He did, however, sign as a free agent for about $150,000 a year. On the day he signed, Brian bought a $50,000 Lexus. Neither his nor Shannon's plans included earning their college degrees—but they had plenty of plans for spending money.

As the story illustrates, there are women out there who may try to trap you by getting pregnant because they are banking on the odds that you'll make it to a league. Therefore, when you lie down with a woman, you must be willing to accept the consequences of your actions. Whether a pregnancy is an accident or planned by only one of the parties involved, there can be nothing accidental about raising a child. We as African-American men can no longer use the excuse that our fathers may have failed to raise us as a reason for not raising our own children. Raising your children is solely your responsibility—it is not the responsibility of the teacher, preacher, or state. It is time for us to rise to the challenge. A great part of this challenge will be recognizing that raising a child is a lifelong commitment requiring sacrifice and dedication. It is imperative that we meet this challenge if there is to be any hope of reversing the current trend of absentee fathers. It's a tough decision, but it's not one that a Real Man ignores. Why? Because a Real Man will do something others won't: admit that he's equally responsible for making babies.

So if you're not ready—or just don't want—to deal with a situation like this, you've got two options: abstain from sex, or, if you choose to indulge, *wear a condom.* Failing to do this means you may be putting your future in someone else's hands.

Five Ways to Keep Her

We would like to say a little about getting your mack on. While in school, you might be blessed to find that special woman, and it would be a shame to lose her because you don't treat her right. We want to offer five key principles to creating a lasting and loving relationship with your woman:

1. **Communication.** Speak freely, openly, and in a timely manner. Accept the fact that there is nothing wrong with sharing your feelings with your woman. Perhaps most important, listen to what she has to say.

2. **Honesty.** Practice this from the outset. Without it, there is no trust; without trust, there really is no relationship.

3. **Respect.** In actions and words, show her affection, admiration, and love. Treat her the way you would want your daughter to be treated.

4. **Equality.** Your woman should be your equal and treated as such. A relationship is like a team sport; each member of this "team" is as important as the other.

5. **Integrity.** Say what you mean and do what you say. If a man doesn't stand by his word, he stands by nothing.

Stick with these principles, but don't get so caught up in your relationship that you lose sight of your overall goals. If your partner is truly down with you, she will understand and respect your desire to better yourself—even if, by doing so, you part with her in the process.

Sexually Transmitted Diseases (STDs)

The most foolproof way to avoid STDs is to abstain from sexual intercourse altogether. For those of you who decide to wait, we say that's perfectly OK. We know others will choose not to abstain for various reasons (raging hormones, newfound freedom, etc.). When you decide to engage in sex, you need to know about the dangers associated with it. If you're not careful, sex can literally become a nasty situation for you and your partner.

Before we get into talking about specific diseases, we want to emphasize that STDs are no joke, and believe us when we say that they can affect you. Check out the impact it had on one young brother:

An Honest Woman

My boy and I were out at a club, when I noticed this fine-ass female dancing all by herself. I mean this girl was Halle Berry fine, and she was dancing just nasty, shaking her big ass. I told my boy, "Dawg, if old girl gives me just five minutes I'm going to hit it before the week is over." I finally got my five minutes and things were going better than expected. We exchanged digits and made plans to hook up the following weekend. The next weekend we had dinner at a little restaurant, and she started talking about her life. She started asking me questions about my views on gay people and other sensitive topics, as though she was feeling me out. Then she said, "I want to tell you something, but I am not sure how you will react." I said, "Just tell me."

She hesitated for a moment and said, "When I had my second child, I lost a lot of blood. I had to have a transfusion, but the blood was tainted and I acquired ARC." I said, "What's that?" She said, "AIDS Related Complex. It's what you get before you actually get full-blown AIDS." I thought, "Oh, shit! How could such a beautiful, healthy-looking woman have AIDS?" She went on to tell me that neither her ex-husband nor the baby had contracted it. But by this point, I was buggin'. She went on to say that the risk of me contracting it was slim, but she felt that I deserved to know. She was pretty convincing, and for a split second I thought, "If I wear two jimmees, I'll be safe." Then I came to my senses and thought, "Hell, no. It ain't worth it." Although I can't remember her name, I respect her a lot for having the courage to let me know so that I could make my own decision. It makes me wonder how many women I have slept with who haven't been so honest. I don't think I personally would or could be as honest.

—T. R. V., Class of 1992

As you can see from the story above, STDs can come in pretty packages. Fellas, this disease does not discriminate. You just never know because you can't always smell it, see it, taste it, assume it, squeeze lemon juice on it, or any of the other ridiculous ways of identifying STDs that young brothers have shared with us.

SEXUAL PARTNER MULTIPLIER

What is a sexual partner multiplier? Say you had unprotected sex with three women in the past year and each one of them has had unprotected sex three times in the last year. Your actual sexual exposure has just increased by at least nine. Each partner had three additional partners, so every time you sleep with one of your partners you were actually sleeping with her and her three partners. That's an example of a sexual partner multiplier.

The following is a brief discussion of some of the STDs that you should be aware of. Some are incurable and deadly, while others are treatable. *All, for the most part, are preventable.*

AIDS (Black Death)

There are numerous theories as to origin of Acquired Immune Deficiency Syndrome. One is that AIDS originated with green monkeys in Africa. This is highly unlikely, because the outbreak of AIDS happened virtually simultaneously throughout the world, not just in parts of Africa. Others say that a promiscuous gay white male started it and spread the deadly disease during a weekend of unprotected sex with numerous other gay men. This, too, is highly unlikely because it is difficult to imagine that one gay male is responsible for the estimated 75 million Africans who are thought to be infected with the disease on the continent. Still others believe that AIDS was created in a laboratory by diabolical men bent on creating a weapon of destruction, which could systematically wipe out an entire race of people.[7] The list goes on and on.

Two things that we know for certain about the disease are that it is **incurable and fatal.** In the

REMEMBER:
Every time you have unprotected sex you are not only sleeping with that person, but you are sleeping with everyone that person has had unprotected sex with, as well as any unprotected sex partners their partners had, and their partner's partners, and so on.

absence of an effective vaccine or cure, your best bets for surviving this devastating illness are abstinence, education, and protection. These are the most effective means you have to avoid contracting and spreading this disease.

Many scientists cautiously agree that the AIDS virus can be transmitted through a number of human body fluids including blood, semen, saliva, tears, urine, breast milk, and vaginal and cervical secretions. Plus, there is evidence indicating that AIDS is transmitted primarily through three methods: sex, whether vaginal, anal, or oral; exposure to infected blood or blood products; and the passing of the viruses from a mother to her unborn child.

CAUTION: Although researchers have learned much about the viruses over the past ten to fifteen years, much is still not known. That could mean that there are additional ways of acquiring the disease. So, please be careful.

We could discuss the symptoms of AIDS, but there's really no point. The bottom line is: if you get it, you die. For those of you who do not fear death, but do fear torture, death by AIDS is typically slow and painful. Sure, there are people who will tell you that having the disease will afford you the opportunity to educate other young people. But wouldn't it be much easier and less painful to educate yourself about this horrific disease, then use your knowledge to warn others?

Let's clear up some of the myths surrounding AIDS:

- Anyone (including YOU) can get it.
- You do not have to be a homosexual, bisexual, or drug addict to get it.

- Everyone is at risk, although some are more than others.

- Jimmees (condoms) will not always prevent the spread.*

- You can not see, smell, hear, or taste it.

* More than one out of every 200 condoms was found to be defective in laboratory tests, a UCLA study has found. The defective condoms either allowed water or air to escape, failed strength tests, or leaked the AIDS virus, the Los Angeles Times reports. All condoms may not be equally effective in preventing [AIDS] transmission," the report said. Nevertheless, it's still safer to use even the worst-scoring condom than no condom at all. (Briefing, "Some condoms leak AIDS," September 17, 1989 issue of the *Chicago Sun-Times*).

As mentioned earlier, abstinence, education, and protection remain the most powerful tools against the spread of this deadly disease. Although studies have shown that not all jimmees are equally effective in preventing the spread (due to small tears, holes, and the occasional major blowout), jimmees are still considered your best bet if you insist on being sexually active. May we suggest, that you *double up* or at least spend the extra change to buy the extra-strength variety. Yeah, we know it's bad enough wearing one, but hopefully your good sense will prevail over your little head's nonsense.

Condom Sense

We know this may sound silly, but we feel compelled to give you some jimmee wearing instructions in case you have never bothered to read the directions. If you don't follow them correctly your jimmee might just blow out.

- Use a jimmee every time you have intercourse or other acts between partners which involve contact with your junk.

Food for Thought:

Do you think Magic, Eazy-E, or any other celebrity who has contracted AIDS was sleeping with butt-ugly women?

- Put the jimmee on after you get erect and prior to intimate contact because lesions, pre-ejaculation secretions, semen, saliva, urine, and other bodily fluids can contain STD organisms.

- Place the jimmee on the head of your penis and unroll or pull it all the way to the base.

- Do not pull the jimmee tightly against the tip of your penis. Leave a space and remove the air from the tip by squeezing the end of the jimmee.

- If you use some type of astro glide, make sure it is water based or silicone based.

- Do not use oil-based lubricants. That means no Vaseline.

- If and after you ejaculate, carefully withdraw the penis while it is still erect. Hold on to the rim as you pull out, so that the jimmee does not slip off.

BURNED

Fortunately, all of the diseases discussed below have a cure, except herpes. Antibiotics will typically squash the problem, if treated early. Make sure that you see a health-care professional for treatment of these ailments. But, as always, prevention is your best cure. A simple ninety-nine cent latex jimmee, properly worn, will go far in preventing you from ever contracting these diseases.

Gonorrhea

Gonorrhea (A.K.A. "the clap"), so named because of the pain men experience when trying to urinate, is an infection caused by the bacterium Neisseria Gonococcus. It is one of the most common STDs. About ten percent to twelve percent of men and about eighty-five percent of women show no apparent signs of the disease. So, as we said before, you can't always see it, smell it, et cetera. Regardless of how embarrassing it might be to tell your partner or partners that you have this disease, you are obligated to do so. If left untreated, gonorrhea can lead to severe problems, especially in women. The disease can cause pelvic inflammatory disease, which can damage the Fallopian tubes and ovaries and ultimately prevent a woman from bearing children. The initial symptoms for men, if any, appear two to ten days after infection. They may include a painful burning sensation when urinating and a nasty penile discharge.

Chlamydia

Chlamydia is an STD which affects the vagina in women and the urethra in men. The urethra is the canal through which you urinate, and also the canal in which sperm is discharged. If you destroy this canal, you might have to have an operation to bypass it and end up urinating in a bag attached to your side. It can also render men sterile and women infertile. Like gonorrhea, chlamydia is often symptomless, but symptoms might include a burning sensation while urinating and frequent trips to the toilet.

Herpes

Herpes Simplex No.1 and No.2 are STDs which still have no cure. That means if you get them, you may be stuck with them for the rest of your life.

Herpes is a general term for a group of viruses (known as herpes viruses) that cause numerous illnesses. There are about five types which can infect you; herpes simplex No.1, which causes nasty cold sores; herpes simplex No. 2, which is primarily responsible for producing blisters and

> **REMEMBER:**
> The more sexual partners you have, the greater the risk of contracting AIDS or any other disease.

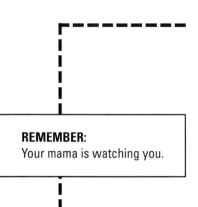

REMEMBER:
Your mama is watching you.

Additional Resources:

AIDS National Information
 Clearinghouse
P.O. Box 6003
Rockville, MD 20850
(800) 458-5231, 342-2437

National Sexually Transmitted
 Diseases Hotline
P.O. Box 13827
Research Triangle Park,
 N.C. 27709
(800) 227-8922

sores around the groin; herpes foster, which causes chicken pox and shingles; Epstein-Barr virus, which causes infectious mononucleosis, known as "mono", and cytomegalovirus, which can cause birth defects in children.

Herpes viruses also have been associated with various cancers in humans. Herpes simplex No.1 and No. 2 should be of greatest concern to you because they are most often acquired through intimate sexual contact, including kissing an infected person.

As mentioned earlier, no cure exists for herpes, but in most cases its severity and frequency can be controlled. If you think you have been infected, seek qualified medical assistance immediately.

Syphilis

Syphilis, although not one of the leading STDs in the United States, still exists. If left untreated, it can cause death. The syphilis bacteria most frequently enters the body through small tears in the skin or through the mouth, rectum, or genital tract while the person is in contact with an in-fected individual. Symptoms usually occur about two to three weeks later. If infected, a man will usually develop a painless sore called a "chan-cre," typically around the penis. The chancre contains a gang of the syphilis bacteria, and is very contagious. Again, seek treatment immediately.

Bibliography: Madhubutti, *Black Men* [1991]; Edwards, Gabrielle, *Coping with Venereal Diseases* [1988]; Levin, SA, *The Clinician's Guide to Sexually Transmitted Diseases*[1987]; Spagna, V. A. and Prior R.B., *Sexually Transmitted Diseases* [1985].

CHAPTER 12. ALMOST ADDICTED

Substance Abuse

For too many people, alcohol and drugs are a way to ease the pain of reality. The following example illustrates exactly what lengths people will go to in order to stop the hurting. We know some of you have equally tragic tales that you could share, and that dwelling on these experiences can get you down. Realize, though, that our goal is not to depress you. Our reason for telling this story, and all the others you'll see in this chapter, is to make sure you know that the temporary escape drugs and alcohol offer is not worth the long-term problems they cause.

> Drugs and drink are at the two arms of the devil with which he strikes his helpless victims into stupefaction and intoxication.
>
> —Mohandas Gandhi

Lost Soul

For me, alcohol was a way to deal with the depression of [his brother] Don's death. I'm not like the average person, I grew up in a different environment altogether. I grew up around pimps, players, and hustlers. When I got mad, I didn't come home and talk about my problems. I hung out and got high. When I got to Detroit, I was bored with football. After Don died, I had lost my motivation to play. Only reason I was playing in the first place was because of Don. He came and took me away from hanging out, and made me play sports. He was my inspiration, and when he died my inspiration was gone.

So my rookie year in Detroit didn't go so well; coaches were trippin' with the playing time. By the time the season was over, I was mad as hell. When I went back to Seattle, and all the hoopla stopped, that's when I really began to deal with grieving over Don. That shit was depressing as hell. No support at all, nobody to turn to. Liquor store was fifteen steps across the street. Spent day in and day out drinking forties, sitting on my couch watching cable. Before I knew it, a week had gone by. That was my way of coping. But now I know that it wasn't the best way. I could have ended up an alcoholic.

—R. R., Class of '86

On a college campus, accessibility to alcohol and drugs is no different than it is for other segments of society. Some of you—whether in junior high, high school, or college—have already heard of or experienced these substances. All of you are at risk of encountering them in the future. In the pages that follow, we will not preach about avoiding drugs. Instead, we will lay out the life experiences of some student-athletes who came before you. The final decision about drug and alcohol use rest with you. We think that after you read this chapter, making the right choice will simply be a matter of *choosing life and prosperity over death and destruction.* It's your call.

Peer Pressure

"Birds of a feather flock together," your mother used to tell you. *"Monkey see, monkey do,"* is another favorite. *"Follow the leader,"* is yet another classic. All of these are adages about people being misguided or misdirected by other individuals.

Fact is, you should rarely be in a peer group that would influence you to go against what you believe to be right and what you believe is in your best interest. If you surround yourself with people who are on the same progressive, productive path as yours, there should not be as much pressure to use drugs or alcohol. If you don't know right from wrong, or what is or isn't good for you, then you had better ask somebody (i.e., success-ful older players, mentors, coaches).

However, a word to the wise. If you make the mistake of hanging out with the wrong crowd and make the wrong decisions at the wrong time, you, my friend, will be at risk of becoming another statistic or another sad story in someone else's book.

Alcohol / Drugs

Remember the quote from Mohandas Gandhi, "Drugs and drink are the two arms of the devil..."? History shows that this assessment couldn't be more accurate. The problems, tragedies, and accidents that often result from alcohol and drug abuse are evidence that humans often behave irrationally when their judgment is chemically impaired. The fact is that anything you put into your body, whether natural herbs or alcoholic beverages, affects your nervous system. Your nervous system is designed to respond on im-pulse, and serves as the body's natural computer, deciding what and where your next move will be. So if your ability to respond—while operating an automobile or simply walking down the street—is impaired, you have placed your own personal safety at risk.

Innocent in High School - Corrupt in College

In high school I was kind of square, I mean I didn't drink or get high. All I did is ball. This all changed my freshmen year in college. My new boys weren't exactly what you would consider to be square, they had been getting lit for years. In just a few weeks I to was getting lit all the time, I mean I could get f---ed up with the best of them. Unfortunately, all that dope smoking impaired my brain cells and when I turned pro I had a real tough time remembering the plays and was eventually cut. To make it even worse I failed to get my degree and now I clean carpets for a living. Just say no!

—M. R. J., Class of '87

The Ride That Changed My Life

Back in 1984, I was a promising young sophomore sprinter anxiously awaiting my opportunity to move up the depth chart. That spring, I thought I would surely get a chance to prove myself to my coach. Spring would come, but I would not be in any shape to run track. As a matter of fact, I was lucky to be alive. It all happened one rainy Saturday night, as I was returning home from a friend's house about 11 o'clock. I'd had a few beers, and maybe even a shot or two, but I felt pretty sober. I was riding my moped when, all of a sudden, a car made a left turn and broadsided me. The last thing I remember is being thrown from the bike; I don't really remember landing. They said the driver of the car was under the influence of alcohol as well. When I woke up in the hospital, the nurse told me that I had been through emergency surgery, and that I was lucky to be alive.

The next day after the pain medicine started to wear off, I had this horrible pain in my hip. That's also when they dropped the bomb on me. I was told that because of my hip damage, my left leg was a full one and one-quarter inch shorter than my right. I would walk with a limp for the rest of my life, and I would *never run track again.* I was devastated. It took a while to get used to the idea of not competing, but I eventually got over that part. The problem is I know that my deformed leg will be with me for the rest of my life.

One less drink for me, maybe one less drink for the other guy, and I would be living a normal life. But now, I'm just another sad story.

—A. W., Class of '87

This example clearly shows that tragedy can strike anytime. The key is to do everything in your power to minimize the possibility of such an event. In the above case, the effects of alcohol on the nervous system played a key role in this accident. We like to think that, had A. W.'s reflexes been in order, his chances of avoiding the accident would have been greater.

Reggie's Story

The night that it happened, I had just flown in from Sacramento, just bought a new jeep that same day. I went by this bar where all the players would hang out on Wednesday nights, right over in the 'hood. I drank a Bud Light and a Tanqueray, then I left and picked up a forty. Me and my boy left the liquor store and was on our way back to the house when all of sudden, *wham*! I got broadsided, and the other car burst into flames. Three teenagers died. I don't remember anything other than the cops trying to ask me questions about what I had to drink. The accident happened a little before midnight, and the police tested my blood alcohol level at about 5 a.m. At that time it (my blood-alcohol level) was legal, but the police attempted to estimate what it must have been at the time of the accident.

They didn't even focus on the teenagers; everyone felt sorry for them because they were dead. Earlier that day, they had gotten kicked out of a church function for being drunk. In the car they found an empty case of beer and two empty fifths of Jack Daniels. Their average blood alcohol level was like a 1.85 or something.

After all of this, I got charged with vehicular manslaughter and got a lawsuit slapped on me. Nobody seemed to worry about what happened to Reggie. My wife had my twins two months premature, my mom developed heart problems because of stress, and I was disabled for over a year while waiting for my neck to heal. All because of some damn alcohol.

—R. R., Class of '86

This is truly a sad story. From the moment of impact, people's lives were altered forever. Alcohol was responsible for the pain, suffering, and the loss of human life. But now it's too late; there is no making up for this mistake. In the words of the fictional character Carlito Brigante in the movie *Carlito's Way*, "There are some lines that you cross in this world, where they ain't no turning back. You gotta go along for the whole ride." This was one of those *lines*, and there ain't no turning back—all because someone made the wrong decision. We hope that the next time your number is called, you will make the right choice. *Please, choose life!*

DRUG ABUSE

If you thought that the horror stories on alcohol abuse were devastating, wait until you read the next few tales of 4D (death, destruction, despair, and devastation). Drugs such as marijuana and cocaine are not only illegal but readily available on and around college campuses. We are here to heighten your awareness of the pitfalls that await you, should you stray down this path of illicit activity. Though you might not be familiar with the stories you are about to read, we guarantee you will never forget them.

The Tragic Death of Don Rogers

The year was 1983, and Don Rogers was an all-American safety out of UCLA. He was drafted in the first round by the Cleveland Browns as one of the top free safeties in the country. Rogers could really lay the hat, and for a big man (six feet two inches tall, 210 pounds), he could cover as well. Thus, it was no wonder that after only his second season, Rogers was being compared to many other great safeties, including Dennis Smith, Kenny Easely, and Ronnie Lott, all destined for the Hall of Fame.

In the spring of 1986, Rogers was planning his wedding and preparing to settle down and start a family. On the eve of his wedding, he ran face first into the pitfalls of his drug abuse. (According to his brother Reggie, Rogers was a real square in college. He had gotten addicted to drugs after he joined the Browns because many of the teammates he hung out with were addicts.) The night of his bachelor party, Rogers—who was using cocaine—suffered a massive heart attack and died en route to a Sacramento hospital. No more career, no more family plans, no more dreams, and most important—no more Don Rogers. His life was tragically lost because, in an instant, he made the wrong decision. It proved to be the last one he would ever make.

Cocaine use caused another high-profile tragedy in 1986. This one would occur some 3,000 miles away in Maryland, a full two weeks before the Don Rogers tragedy. Len Bias, an All-American forward at the University of Maryland and the Boston Celtics' first draft pick, was partying on the night after the draft. He and his friends celebrated his success into the early morning hours. Later, Bias returned to his dormitory to try to get some sleep, but began having seizures at 6:30 a.m. Two teammates attempted to resuscitate him, then called for emergency assistance. The paramedics who transported Bias to the hospital kept his heart beating by artificial means. He arrived at the hospital in full cardiac arrest, and never regained consciousness. Len Bias never knew what hit him.

The Aaron Pryor Story

Aaron Pryor was an amateur boxer from Cincinnati who had won 204 of 220 fights. In 1980, he won the Junior Welterweight Championship and made millions of dollars. After defeating Alexis Arguello for a second time, Pryor returned to Miami. In Miami, he tried crack for the first time. He liked it so much that he did not want anything else. Pryor won his last championship in 1985, and retired shortly afterward. His crack habit got so bad that when he ran out of money, he began to trade cars, clothing, even furniture for the drug. He soon lost all of his money, real estate, and just about everything he owned. Aaron Pryor had bottomed out.

In March of 1991, he was arrested and convicted of drug use, then served three months in the state penitentiary. After his release, Pryor got hooked on crack again and ended up homeless. He spent his day standing on street corners and shadowboxing for handouts from people who pointed at him and laughed. Other times he sparred in alleys with tough guys from the street who wanted to see how they stacked up against the former champion.

Pryor's life did not turn around until he developed bleeding stomach ulcers and got deathly sick. After about three weeks of being bedridden at his girlfriend's place, Pryor got up one Sunday and walked to church. The New Friendship Church changed his life and probably saved it. Aaron Pryor currently trains fledgling boxers for $350 per week in Cincinnati. His life went from rags to riches, to drugs to rags. Now, he is richer than ever; he has become rich in spirit.

—**Source:** Sports Illustrated, Feb. 13, 1995, "Pryor Restraint."

As you can see, cocaine abuse literally killed two people and nearly ruined the life of another. All three of these men were once considered strong, virile, invincible athletes. Yet, like other human beings, they were not immune to this biological addiction.

The question for you, then, is what decision would you have made in these situations? Have you been in similar situations and made the wrong choice? Could we be writing about your mistakes instead of someone else's in our next volume? Only you know the answers to these questions. As the characters Hanz and Franz from Saturday Night Live would say, "Believe us now or listen to us later." If you select the wrong answers, you sure as hell better get help. Remember, though, that the best way to prevent addiction is to abstain from using drugs or alcohol. Otherwise, *you* could be the star of the next sad story.

STEROIDS

The use of anabolic steroids has been prevalent in college and professional athletics for a long time. However, only in the last ten years have the covers been pulled off of this illegal and dangerous substance abuse problem.

One of the earliest cases to shed the spotlight on steroids involved Steve Courson, a former Pro-Bowl guard on the Pittsburgh Steelers' 1979 Super Bowl championship team. Later, while with the Tampa Bay Buccaneers, Steve confessed to heavy steroid use, particularly during his early years in Pittsburgh. So when the news of his having a stretched and dilated heart came out, those closest to him were not surprised. His cardiologist theorized that excessive use of anabolic steroids possibly triggered an unnatural growth process in his heart and caused abnormal dilation of the heart muscle. Unless he began treatment and immediately ceased playing football, his doctor said, Courson would be at risk of having a massive heart attack. In the words of Dr. Richard Rosenbloom, Courson's cardiologist, "His long-term prognosis is better with a heart transplant than it is his present condition." Courson did retire from football and began treatment while a search was launched for an organ donor. The latest information on Courson was that he had lost 120 pounds of his playing weight, but was optimistic about finding a donor.[8]

The Lyle Alzado Story

Former defensive tackle and All-Pro, Lyle Alzado starred with the Denver Broncos and L. A. Raiders for a combined fourteen years. After his football career ended, Alzado confessed not only to prolific steroid use, but to also taking injections of animal growth hormones. The use of these hormones, combined with the steroids, caused the brain cancer that eventually lead to his death in 1992. Alzado was once asked, "Was the opportunity to play and compete in professional football worth abusing your body and cutting your life short?" He replied, " I have lived a good life, and I realized one of my dreams in playing in the NFL, but **hell, no,** it was not worth it. I realize now that nothing is more precious than the gift of life. But now it is too late." Weeks before his death, a frail Alzado said, "If what I have become doesn't scare you off steroids, nothing will."

—**Source:** *Sports Illustrated,* July 8, 1991, A Doctor's Warning Ignored

Courson and Alzado had a strong desire to succeed athletically, just as you probably do. So have many other steroid abusers like them. They were willing to go to any lengths to achieve athletic success for themselves, up to and including risking their own lives. What did they attain? Wealth? Fame and fortune? Yes, but only

REMEMBER:
Drugs and alcohol are not the answer to your problems. They only become a part of the problem.

Additional Resources:

The National Clearinghouse for Drug Abuse Information
5600 Fisher Lane
Room 10A-43
Rockville, MD 20857

National Association of State Alcohol and Drug Abuse Directors
444 North Capital Street Suite 530
Washington, DC 20001
(202) 783-6868

for a short time. They will be remembered for their terminal medical problems and, in the case of Alzado, a premature death. Are you willing to take the same risks? We suspect your answer is, "Absolutely not." Will you make the right choice? Only time will tell. Think twice, brother, because you only get one shot at life.

COPING

Dealing with the sometimes harsh nature of reality can sometimes be difficult for even the strongest person. People cope in different ways, but some of the coping methods you have learned might not be good for you. In dealing with the problems of everyday life, you will find that a method for coping will prove to be very helpful. This method does not include escapism through drugs or alcohol. It is very important that you learn to deal with the variety of feelings that humans experience, from happiness to depression. It would be helpful if you could learn to identify what you are feeling, and deal with it accordingly. Don't ignore your feelings, because when you do they return to the surface in new and more dangerous forms. Deal with them as they come along. Find someone to discuss your problems with. Form support groups and/or talk to the minister at your church. We have also included a list of phone numbers that you can call for assistance. Find a responsible way to cope with reality.

CHAPTER 13. YOU AND SCOOP

Media Relations
by Art Tiel

Not How It Looks

A newspaper reporter, skeptical about why a star basketball player was demoted, sought the truth from one of the star's teammates.

"Do you want the truth," the student-athlete said, "or can I tell you what the coaches told us to say?" The reporter said he always preferred the truth. "I understand that," the athlete said, "but can you under-stand my need to keep my scholarship?"

The reporter understood, and reluctantly backed away from the student-athlete, and a good story. What he did have was another example of the conflict between big-time college sports and the truth.

One of the great ironies of college life is that, while students are taught to question authority in every other department on campus, the athletic department teaches absolute and unswerving respect for authority. Coaches hold so much power over the athletic fate of their players that their beliefs become mandatory for the team. In the above case, it is doubtful that the coach would or could have pulled the player's scholarship. But that reality is often lost on the typical student-athlete. What he does know is that an honest answer will gain him the reporter's respect, and subject him to punishment from the coach and abuse from his teammates.

> The price that one has to pay in public life is that of being misquoted, misrepresented, and misunderstood.
>
> —Dr. Martin L. King, Jr.

The relationship between college athletes and media, particularly in larger cities, is often awkward. The universities and athletic programs have a large financial interest in seeing their teams and individuals portrayed in the most flattering light. Positive images help sustain fund-raising, attract highly qualified faculty and coaches, and make athletic recruiting easier.

That is why many schools spend large sums on sports-information departments filled with university employees whose primary task is to crank out tons of neutral to positive information about the school's athletes and teams, particularly the revenue-producing sports of football and men's basketball.

Most of the time, reporters turn this information into stories for newspapers, radio, and TV, supplemented with their own interviews and research. Inevitably, there will be issues that a university doesn't want to publicly discuss: losing streaks, coach firings, player disputes, drug use, assaults, academic failings, and the usual litany of NCAA rules violations.

In fact, relatively few among the many thousands of scholarship athletes in the United States are involved in breaking laws, rules, or codes of conduct. But since so much media attention is directed at sports, especially college sports, it seems as if every sport at every school is consumed by scandal.

Clearly, that is not the case. But because the few problem athletes are known by the many, it is inevitable that the uninvolved athlete will be sought out for opinions and information. That's the source of the awkwardness: tell the truth, as your mother always insists, or shut up—even lie—as the coach insists.

That is a moral debate for which there is no easy answer. Most athletes, feeling the pressure to be a part of the team and the university, decline to help the media. That is a right that can never be denied. One consequence, however, is that maintaining this silence creates an us-versus-them conflict that breeds resentment and hostility. In the end, neither party is well served.

But an athlete who is media-savvy can blunt the consequences of those difficult moments by cultivating relationships with media members. A respectful, rather than adversarial, relationship with reporters provides the athlete with a crucial advantage: *the benefit of the doubt.*

Regardless of how coaches may want to demonize reporters, most reporters are simply out to find a story that will please editors, readers, viewers, and listeners. They do not seek to make athletes or programs look bad, nor do they seek conflict. They want to be liked and to be treated fairly.

FIRST IMPRESSIONS

Developing a good media personality is often very little more than using the same social skills one employs when seeking to impress any stranger:

- Make and keep eye contact.
- Offer a handshake like you mean it. (When in doubt, keep the handshake standard.)
- Listen for a reporter's first name, and use it once or twice answering questions.
- Don't forget to smile. This isn't a visit to the dentist or to the police.

What may be unusual for some athletes in the interview experience is sharing details of one's life to a stranger, and subsequently, to many thousands more strangers.

Remember: you are being sought because you are a special person, someone of accomplishment whose actions are of interest to many people. Recall your feelings as a youngster, when you did or saw something special and couldn't wait to tell your buddies. As a college athlete, it's not advisable to jump up and down and giggle in the fashion of an eight-year-old, but you can convey an enthusiasm about yourself and your situation that will always reflect well in any story.

Trust is always an elusive part of an athlete's relationship with the media. Rarely is it given during the first meeting, by either side. But through the course of a college career, there is a good chance that an athlete will encounter the same local reporters again and again. If there has been a mutually respectful relationship from the beginning, chances are great that the reporter will feel empathy for you and may well become an ally and even a friend, although policy at most newspapers discourages friendships between reporters and sources.

An athlete should work toward a goal of friendliness. Spotting a familiar reporter, calling him by name, kidding him about his tie (or lack thereof) or a story of his is the sort of easy relationship that will almost always work in the athlete's favor.

Some players always seem to pull the "pub," even beyond their accomplishments. Why? Because they tend to be thoughtful, funny, or complete in their answers to media questions. If they are all three, you might see them someday doing color commentary on one of the networks.

Among the worst things you can do in an interview is to be abrupt, or take yourself overly seriously. It's easy to do early in a career, overwhelmed as most freshmen are with college. But it's doubtful you act that way among your friends. If you depart from the conventional athletic department wisdom that reporters are out to get you, and recognize that they can be as helpful as a good teacher or a favorite uncle, it becomes easy to be frequently quoted on a variety of team topics.

Giving away team secrets is definitely a no-no, but there are always plenty of offbeat things that happen to you or your teammates that make for good anecdotes. These are short, often funny stories that lend some insight into a person or a situation. Reporters love anecdotes like grandkids love Grandpa's tales. Anecdotes humanize subjects, making the reader of the story identify with the athlete or team. You will be asked frequently to comment on another player instead of yourself, so having a good story about how he tried to talk his way around being late to practice, or how he had to leave by his dorm-room window because his door was taped shut will always pay off in a good media relationship.

A CLOSER LOOK

If you are the subject of an in-depth interview, realize that the reporter is seeking information that perhaps only your family or girlfriend knows about you. It is always a difficult judgment call to know how much to share, but realize that ninety-nine percent of stories by local reporters will cast any personal, family, or legal difficulties in a supportive fashion. There will always be some readers or viewers appalled by some disclosures, but the vast majority will commend an athlete for sharing the ordeals as well as the triumphs. Nearly all reporters, as well as a team's followers, have more tolerance for college athletes than for professional athletes.

Some young athletes have expressed confusion, likely encouraged by coaches, over the role of reporters. As in, are you with us or against us? The fact is, the majority of reporters are neither.

There are some notable exceptions: the local radio and TV broadcast crews are typically homers, as are most TV reporters. So are some newspaper writers, particularly those in predominantly college towns where speaking critical words against Enormous State University can result in large rocks being thrown through picture windows.

Generally, most reporters in larger cities and any reporter who wants a future in newspapers are officially neutral when it comes to the local team. Journalism rules dictate that they cannot care one way or another about the outcome of the game. The object is to report on and explain the game and team, not lead cheers.

Deep down, reporters tend to pull for the team they cover, although sometimes old college loyalties may provoke hostile feelings about a rival. But don't expect an admission of feelings from a reporter, particularly in front of his peers. And never ask a reporter who he wants to see win a game: his professional objectivity is a valued part of his credibility.

BAD PUBLICITY

When there is what you perceive to be a negative story about you or your team, it's important to know that all but the most high-profile scandals fade quickly from the memory of the public and media. Nevertheless, it's always tough to see your face on TV or name in print connected with an unpleasant story. The fact is, if you are at all prominent, an unfavorable story will happen at least once, perhaps several times. That's not necessarily personal; it just human nature and the law of averages. Be prepared.

Each circumstance is likely so different that it's hard to generalize about a response. But the easiest thing to do is also the least productive:

blame the media. If someone publishes out-and-out lies, you and your school should find a lawyer. But if a writer expresses an opinion—particularly a columnist, whose job is all about opinions—that slights or disses you or your team, realize that actions speak louder than any words of confrontation or opposition.

Remember, too, that while factual errors shouldn't be tolerated by the reporter or the subject of the story, a reporter's printed or broadcast opinion about who will win the game, which team does or doesn't deserve a bowl bid or tournament selection, or who is or isn't a blue-chip recruit, is not necessarily an insult or a compliment. It is one person's opinion given to others. That's the lifeblood of spectator sports. The fact that people know enough about you and your team to care one way or the other is flattering, even if they don't agree. The worst thing in spectator sports is apathy—not caring. The give-and-take about sports is a big reason our society savors and elevates athletes. It's fun, and everyone is not only entitled to an opinion, they are encouraged to share it. *Don't take it personally.*

If you can't help but take it personally, don't add to your troubles by making a crusade against the reporter. In that sort of fight, the old rule has always been: *the guy with the ink wins.* Demonstrate in the arena or on the field. To dismiss a reporter by saying, "You don't know what you're talking about because you've never played the game," is like saying someone can't tell the difference between a good egg and a bad egg because he isn't a chicken.

EXPRESS YOURSELF

A difficulty for some young African-American athletes is expressing themselves to white journalists and the mostly white public. This is not as large an issue as it used to be, but some college followers have antiquated, hostile views. Some athletes feel to "talk and act white" to please an audience is a sell-out; others go along and feel uncomfortable. The fact is, the only mistake in this area is to be phony, because phoniness will eventually come back to haunt you, either with

High School Athletes

At the high school level, some players and coaches think a sympathetic reporter can be influential in obtaining a scholarship. Years ago, that sometimes may have been the case. But modern recruiting techniques coupled with a network of scouts have virtually eliminated the reporter as a well-informed source of a player's college potential. Certainly a favorable story about an obscure but talented player can't hurt. But any coach or player or parent who tries to coax a reporter to do a story for selfish reasons will, more often than not, alienate the reporter.

A feature story on a high school player needs to have some drama, fun, uniqueness, or unusual achievement to gain play in the increasingly crowded sports page. If someone connected with the player can provide such information to a reporter without telling the reporter how to do his or her job, the chance for coverage increases.

teammates or the public. You are who you are, and you have no obligation to modify your behavior because of a few unenlightened people. Such people are not worth pleasing, even if they have some influence over your academic and athletic career, or your personal life. (See Chapter 4, In Transition.)

However, courtesy, common sense, and basic manners have nothing to do with race. Those virtues will serve well in any situation. The key is to not anticipate an awkward or adversarial attitude from a white journalist until the reporter demonstrates it. As everywhere, there are bigots in the media. From this reporter's view, they seem to be relatively few. Many of the slights that can occur come from ignorance, not hostility.

Perhaps you would be surprised to learn that you can make a media ally for life if, upon discovering in a news story what you perceive to be poor, improper, or misleading information that has a racial undertone, you seek out the writer or broadcaster and say something like: "You may or may not know this, but be aware that the next time this comes up, some people may read what you wrote in a way you didn't mean . . . "

Nine times out of ten, the reporter will be equal parts embarrassed and grateful. No reporter who wants a future can afford to make many mistakes of insensitivity. A non-confrontational approach allows the reporter to apologize and recognize the error without getting defensive, and it elevates you in his or her eyes.

The world is awash in an explosion of media, and sports are a big part of it. For a student-athlete to be cold, bored, or even confrontational toward reporters is to abuse a tool that can create multiple opportunities in athletics and beyond it. There are times that the media can be exasperating, overbearing, and just plain stupid. But remember—it's like that in anything. Start with two of the easiest virtues in the world, a smile and some enthusiasm, and your media personality already has a first down at midfield.

notes:

Agent Selection Process

featuring Kenneth L. Shropshire

Agent to the Stars?

In the mid-1980s, an agent named Norby Walters and his partner Lloyd Bloom signed fifty-eight college football and basketball players to management contracts.

Federal prosecutors later would charge that Mr. Walters and his partner used money, trips and concert tickets to sign the collegians, thus inducing them to break college rules on eligibility. If players changed their minds, according to evidence unearthed by Federal investigators, Mr. Walters talked of breaking legs and said that some of his money came from the Mob. In other words, if you reneged, you got beat down.

—Source: *New York Times*, Jan. 26, 1992

Education takes place in the combination of the home, the community, the school and the receptive mind.

—Harry Edwards

Obviously, Walters and Bloom never saw *New Jack City*. That movie put everybody on notice that brothers aren't putting up with that mob nonsense anymore. In the above case, kids started reneging and testifying and the two men were eventually convicted of racketeering. We know this for a fact because some of our boys actually testified. The point is that if you are fortunate enough to make it to a league, there will be many people jocking you and some of these people will try to beat you.

THE RULES

NCAA rules <u>do not</u> prohibit contact with agents or their representatives. However, there are many people who wish they did. The fact is, though, you can jeopardize your college eligibility if you agree (orally or in writing) to be represented by an agent or anyone wanting to market your athletic abilities. It does not matter if the agreement is dated after your final college game.

The NCAA <u>does</u> prohibit you or anyone related to you from receiving benefits or gifts from agents or their representatives. Doing so can cause you to lose your eligibility. If you lose your eligibility, you will not be the only one who will be harmed. Your school's athletic program, recruiting efforts, and reputation will also be damaged. If you are approached and you are unsure about the appropriateness of any agent's behavior, talk to your coach or call the NCAA. If you are fortunate enough to make it to a league, do not jeopardize your success by taking things from unscurpulus agents. It ain't worth it. *Patience, my brother.*

NCAA ADJUSTMENTS

To help kids avoid people like Walters and Bloom, the NCAA in 1984 began to permit schools to establish panels to counsel athletes in such areas as selecting agents. To address this issue, we spoke with our boy Kenneth Shropshire[9], author of *Agents of Opportunity*. Ken is a staunch believer in the use of some type of selection committee when choosing an agent, whether it be formally organized by the school or picked by the student-athlete.

" It (agent contacts) is the number one problem that exists in intercollegiate athletics today."

—Terry Donahue, former head football coach UCLA

Here's what he told us:

Vince: Ken, what should a kid do when trying to decide on an agent?

Ken: In selecting a sports agent, the student athlete must take charge.

Vince: What do you mean by taking charge?

Ken: I mean that he is in control of the process and the final decision, but not necessarily the day-to-day mechanics of what can be an arduous process. To successfully be in charge, the student-athlete must have an agent selection system in place prior to the end of his final season. The key is an organized process and trusted individuals, including family members where possible.

Vince: What are some of the things a kid should consider when putting together a selection committee?

Ken: In discussing this issue with NFL Hall of Famer and sports agent Kellen Winslow, we developed a list of "Ten Things to Consider" before moving forward in putting in place an agent selection process and selecting a committee:

1. How will you handle the barrage of prospective agents seeking to represent you? Do you have a plan?

2. What objective standards will you apply to the selection process?

3. Who will assist you in the decision-making process?

4. Does the agent have to be an attorney?

5. Does the agent's prior playing experience provide any beneficial insight?

6. Do you care about who the agent represented before and whether the relationship continued after the athlete's playing career was over?

7. Are the cultural makeup, background, and sensitivity of the agent important to you? If so, why?

8. Do you want the agent to handle your financial affairs? If not, do you have alternative plans that include working with qualified professionals?

9. What are your plans for life after your professional career?

10. Do you prefer that the agent has contacts for marketing and endorsement opportunities?

Before asking others to do any work, the student-athlete must be able to answer the above questions and convey these answers to those assisting in screening.

Vince: How involved should the student-athlete be in the process?

Ken: This is another initial decision that must be made by the student-athlete. He can do anything from a small amount to all of the work directly, or he may choose to delegate a great deal of the work to committee members and limit his involvement to getting to know the agent and determining his comfort level with him or her, and making that final decision.

Vince: It's unfortunate that during this process many kids become so caught up that they lose focus of their academic and athletic objectives.

Ken: That's right. It is important to know that the selection process can also be used to prevent distractions during a student-athlete's final playing season. The athlete who takes charge can establish the guidelines for the agent. The first time a contact is received from an agent the athlete can simply say, "Thank you for your interest. At this point, I am requesting that all agents submit material to (designated person). At the end of the season, we will review all materials and contact those that we will interview further." I often recommend that athletes actually have cards printed up on where agents can send materials. If the prospective agent can not follow those directions, then you know he won't be good at taking directions from you later on. That should be one of the considerations in the end.

Vince: What size committee should a kid have? I remember when I was working for an agency, we went before a committee of one and after giving our spiel, the only thing the guy wanted to know was how much money was in it for him if he got the kid to sign with us. The bad thing about it was that the kid really trusted the guy.

Ken: The committee can be of any size, consisting of between one and probably no more than five people. If there is a family attorney or trusted family member, it may be helpful to have him or her involved in some of the final interviews. This may help with the trust factor.

Vince: What responsibilities should the kid ask the committee to have?

Ken: The student-athlete may ask the committee to sift through materials and phone calls and give him the top ten (or whatever number) to review. The committee will select this group based on the guidelines the student-athlete provides. Interviews can then be set up with the agents so they can come in and give formal presentations.

Vince: What type of questions should the kid and the committee members ask of the potential agents?

Ken: Again, Kellen and I put our heads together and came up with the following list of questions that should be answered.

1. Are you certified by the appropriate unions?

2. How many players do you currently represent?

3. What assistance do you offer in postcareer development?

4. Do you or does your agency handle the financial affairs of the client? If so, who does the day-to-day work and what are their professional credentials?

5. Did you ever play sports on the collegiate level? Did you ever play on the professional level?

6. Do you have any professional affiliations?

7. Do you do this full time? If not, what else do you do?

8. Are you now being sued or have you ever been sued by a former client? If so, why and what was the outcome of the litigation?

9. Have you ever sued or are you currently suing a client and if so, why? (Attorneys should also be asked if they have been the subject of any disciplinary action.)

10. What marketing plan do you have in mind for the national and local marketplaces?

11. When I need service after the signing of my contract, will you be my personal contact person on a daily basis?

12. Will you be the person who actually negotiates my contract? If not, who will?

Vince: OK, you or your committee have asked these questions. Then what?

Ken: Once these questions are asked of all the candidates, there should be three final steps.

First, call references provided by the agent. This should preferably be a mix of active and retired clients. Second, call the respective players' associations to see if they have additional information regarding the agent. Finally, visit the top choices. Nothing should be signed during the visit. The final selection should be made in consultation with the committee. But, remember, the ultimate choice belongs to the student-athlete.

Vince: Asante Sana (thank you), my brother.

One Like Me

The agent arena for years has been dominated by white males, but African-Americans are finally starting to make significant advancements into this elite area. And why shouldn't we, since African-Americans represent the bulk of the players in the leagues? Larry Anderson of the AR Sports agency says that racism is still a concern for Black agents. He recalls that when he was starting out, he saw white agents advise athletes against dealing with Black agents because management wouldn't take them seriously.[10] Today, general managers want to win games and will negotiate with whomever they have to to get the deal done.

The bottom line is that with all thing being equal (competency, character, etc.,) choose an agent—regardless of race, creed, or color—who has your best interest at heart. Don't choose someone just because he looks like you, but because he can do the job well. However, recognize that there are many qualified African-American agents, financial advisers, tax accountants, attorneys, etc. in need of your business. Their families need to eat, too. We think Bill Strickland, president of basketball operations at IMG, said it best when addressing why he has been so successful. "You have to be wary of thinking that your heritage alone is enough to attract athletes. You're dealing with someone's livelihood. If you screw up, it's going to be magnified."

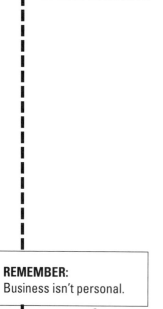

REMEMBER:
Business isn't personal.

The Agent's Responsibilities

After selecting an agent, what is his/her responsibility to you? Remember that the agent works for you. Unfortunately some agents have become so large in their own minds that they see themselves as more important than their clients. At the same time, recognize that an agent should be more knowledgeable about some things than you are—that's why the person was hired. We're not saying that you don't need to understand what the agent does. You'd better understand it, because his actions could leave you broke. But remember, if your agent is unable to explain things (be it financial or otherwise) in a manner which you can reasonably understand, you need to get rid of that agent. If you don't understand concepts such as tax shelters, pork belly futures, whole life insurance, etc., don't invest in them.

We talked to another one of our boys, attorney Fred Whitfield, about an agent's responsibilities. Whitfield is the former director or F.A.M.E, an agency that represents the likes of Michael Jordan, Patrick Ewing, and Juwan Howard.

Andre: What is the responsibility of the agent?

Fred: The first and foremost function of an agent is to negotiate the professional contract for his client. Since most athletes have probably never seen a standard form contract, it is apparent that most of them need guidance and leadership in negotiating the best possible compensation package. In addition, the agent should be able to assist in the management of financial affairs, limit the player's tax liability, counsel the player on numerous subjects, market the athlete, resolve various disputes in which the player may be involved, and help set and achieve realistic long and short term goals for the athlete.

Vince: Let me add one. Any good agent should also be concerned with the public image of his clients. If for no other reason, the player's image will add to his own personal wealth. If a kid has problems with drugs or alcohol, it would behoove the agent to help that kid out, because the agent will get paid only if the kid remains in the league. If a kid is a superstar, but can't speak very well, the agent should see to it that the kid gets linguistic help. It amazes me that some agents don't recognize the benefits of helping their guys develop and maintain a good public image.

Andre: More specifically, what should be the agent's objective in negotiating contracts?

Fred: Every agent should have two very important goals in mind when negotiating a playing contract. One, get as much money as possible, and two, get as much security as possible.

Andre: What do you mean by security?

Fred: I mean that it is not advisable for a player to accept money in lieu of guarantees. The optimum situation is a combination of high dollars and substantial security. Security on a playing contract may be either in the form of a skill guarantee or an injury guarantee. A skill guarantee assures the player that he will be paid regardless of whether his team feels his abilities have decreased to an unacceptable level. An injury guarantee assures a player that he will be paid the remainder of his contract even if he is injured such that he can not adequately perform and play on his team.

Andre: Why wouldn't an agent secure guarantees for his clients?

Fred: Since many agents are paid a percentage up-front out of their client's signing bonuses, many seek to negotiate the highest dollar figure possible, without guarantees. Bargaining away a player's security interest in lieu of a few more dollars is certainly not in the best interest of the player.

Vince: Let me add one more. A good agent, from the start of a relationship with a player, should actively show concern and implement a plan for the kid's life after athletics. After all, we are talking about a career which lasts, on average, two to three years. If an agent doesn't take this initiative, then you may want to reconsider signing with him.

Andre: Thanks, Fred.

About Fees

Years ago, agents could charge whatever they wanted to for their services. Oftentimes, this did not include the best of service. This has all changed as player unions have set commission limits of four percent to five percent of the negotiated contract amount above the minimum salary. Due to the competitive nature of the business, some agents will charge nothing to negotiate your deal as long as they have the right to pitch the endorsement deals. You may want to be skeptical of these people, because as the saying goes, *"You get what you pay for."*

There has been much debate over whether it is better to pay by the hour or by percentage of the contract amount. If you pay by the hour, the agent may be tempted to negotiate forever, so that his fees will be higher. Thus, the chance of losing out on a good deal exists. On the other hand, if you pay by commission, the agent may have incentive to do things that are also not in your best interest, like forgoing guarantees to get a higher dollar amount. It's a difficult call. Ultimately, it should be your decision on how you want to pay.

Whatever method you choose, it is extremely important that you fully understand the nature of the fee arrangement. It may also be good to compare the services offered in relation to the fees charged and to possibly use this in making your final decision on who you want to go with. Once again, *"You get what you pay for."*

Finally, many agents want their money taken out of your signing bonus as soon as you get it. This type of agent may be shortsighted and have little concern as to your future well-being because he has gotten his. Ideally, you should attempt to negotiate terms with your agent that will best benefit your particular financial situation.

Some agents may get upset about what we're going to say next, but here it is: *Don't allow your agent to also handle your money—even if the agent has "in-house experts" to handle players' money (unless they are extremely qualified)*. We base this advice on the actions of unscrupulous agents who have, unfortunately, screwed up things for the rest. If you think about it, it doesn't make sense to give another person access to all aspects of your life. Besides, for some strange reason, too many agents think they know about things they have no expertise in. For example, some agents think they are experts in tax shelters, but they aren't practicing tax attorneys or accountants. For whatever reason, some agents try to play Mr. Know-It-All or the Jack-of-All-Trades.

Invest your money with competent and responsible professionals who handle finances for a living. Many banks and investment houses offer money management services to potentially high-wealth individuals like yourself. Their services can include many of the following: asset management, budget and money management, income collection, tax planning, bill payments, property management, business advisory, valuation services, and retirement planning. These companies are independent of your agent and possess deep pockets. In essence, they can be held accountable for the mismanagement of your money. That means that if you end up broke, you can sue the institution that handled your money and, if you win the case, the institution can afford to pay you. On the other hand, an agent might not be able to pay damages if you sue him and win the case.

Kareem, Don Sutton, Tony Gwynn, Tony Dorsett, Ralph Samson, etc. have all been guilty at one time or another of allowing others to be responsible for their financial well being, and they got took.

About Marketing

An effective agent should be able to evaluate his client's marketability, then match the client with the appropriate endorsement possibilities. The agent knows that not every athlete will get a high-profile Reebok or Nike contract, so it is his job to explore all possible endorsements—even appearances at trading card shows or auto dealerships. These low-profile appearances are not necessarily low-income opportunities, especially when the agent has negotiated fees for several appearances. In other words, the money

About Finances

The professional athlete spends all of his life preparing for the day that he turns from amateur to professional. If only he would spend one hour a week preparing for his new found wealth.

—Earl A. Layne, Vice President, Star Bank Professional Sports Group from these opportunities can add up. Besides, getting out in the community might allow you to form relationships that can further your endeavors after your playing years.

When seeking an agent, look for one who employs people whose sole job is to secure endorsement opportunities for clients. However, all the marketing muscle in the world will not result in endorsement deals if you don't have yourself together. Tony Rome, Director of Athlete Marketing at ProServ, says, "An athlete's marketability is impacted, positively or negatively, by his or her ability to communicate convincingly to the media and public." Denise Harrington, of Harrington & Associates Communication Training[11], adds, "If athletes are to gain the endorsement dollars they are looking for, it's critical they know how to interact with the media. Companies want players that are articulate, have a personal image, and are knowledgeable about what they do."

About Life Afterward

Recognize that the careers of most professional athletes are relatively short. Although the money may be good while you are playing, most guys will have to find careers after athletics in order to keep the cash flowing. So a good agent, from the start of your relationship, will make sure that all decisions are made with this eventuality in mind. Addressing issues such as degree completion, off-season work experience, business skills development, image consulting, etc., is a must if you hope to transform your athletic experiences into a viable career after athletics. More than likely, a good agent is also concerned about helping you become the best businessperson possible so that the two of you will have the option of doing business together later. There's absolutely nothing wrong with an agent having a vested interest in your succeeding; that just means he/she will work even harder to help you reach this goal. You are clearly the winner here. Even if you have the misfortune of choosing an agent who doesn't have these concerns, it is still your responsibility to prepare yourself. Basically, that means living your life as though your career may end tomorrow. "A fool and his money," the old saying goes, "are soon parted." When it comes to money, you simply can't afford to be a fool.

Additional Resource:

A Career in Professional Athletics
The NCAA
6201 College Boulevard
Overland Park, KS 66211-2422
(913) 339-1906

notes:

ABOUT CULTURE

by Warde Manuel Doctoral Candidate

As an African-American athlete your skin color will always be your preeminent characteristic in the eyes of the media, coaches, and fans. This is evident from the structure of the athletic environment to the comments that are made in the media. Given the experiences of African-American athletes historically, you must be conscious of the history of the sports you play. This context will help you understand that professional sports will not be a viable career choice for the overwhelming majority of African- American athletes.

Although professional sports provide athletes with some financial rewards, it tends to lull many away from attaining the education and skills needed to support a family. The diversionary nature of athletics leads some of my friends to remark upon the inequity in college sports. Their argument focuses on the differences between the amount of money that the athletic department made while they were playing and the value of their scholarships. Ironically, all of my friends who have commented in this manner have not graduated. Given the past and present graduation rates for African-American athletes, the ultimate payoff is not professional sports, but rather a college degree. This is not to say that being a professional athlete is not an admirable goal, it was one of mine, but it should be placed in the proper perspective so that there is a true balance between academic, athletic, and life goals.

In the classroom and on the playing field you are often defined by the color of your skin. There are many stereotypes of African-American athletes. Regardless of the sport in which you participate or the position that you play the connotation is that you are fast, agile, and quick. People often assume that you were accepted at your university only because you are athletically gifted, which implies that you are not academically qualified to compete. Overall, the graduation rates of African-American athletes are significantly lower than those of your white counterparts, but higher than those of the general African-American student population. The latter is an important comparison to understand in the context of resources. The main reason that African-American students do not graduate from a university is because of the lack of money, therefore comparing African-American athletes with the general African-American student population is an unfair comparison.

Realize that you should be graduating at the same level as white student-athletes regardless of your background. Most major sports programs have the resources available to help student-athletes, but do not have those same resources available to the general student population.

The college athletic experience is comprised of two full time jobs: athletics and education. Most students who attend four year universities are full-time students. Many do not have to work in order to pay for their education, some take out loans, some are financed by their parents, and others receive some type of scholarship. Athletes, who are on full scholarships never receive a bill for tuition, room, or board, but they must participate in athletics to maintain their scholarships. As a former student-athlete who received an $80,000 education, I realized the importance of my athletic scholarship when I married my wife and experienced the pain of helping her pay back student loans. Looking back I realize that those student-athletes who did not take advantage of their educational opportunities are either currently unemployed, still attempting to make the pros, or working in a job that does not make use of their college experiences. You must not make the same mistake.

Your ability to know who you are coming into college will help you to understand the person you will be when you leave the college. College is not for everyone, but more people benefit from college than from professional sports. The benefits of college are long term (40-50 years longer) than professional athletics (3 year average). Professional athletics can provide you with a good start only if you have something to finish. The great thing about college athletics is that even if you don't become a professional athlete—it still provides you with a great start.

SELF DEVELOPMENT

Reading List

About Communication

Six Weeks to Words Power, W. Fank
1100 Words You Need to Know, Barron's
How to Build a Better Vocabulary, M. Nurnberg

About Current Events

Black Enterprise
Essence
News Week
U.S. News
Wall Street Journal

About Finances

Investing for Dummies, E. Tyson
Smart Money Moves for African Americans, K. Boston
The WSJGuide to Understanding Money, K. Morris
The Only Investment Guide, A. Tobias

About Manhood

Black Men, H. Madhubuti
Boys to Men, G. Benjamin
Bringing the Black Boy to Manhood, N. Hare
Street Soldier, J. Marshall

About Networking

African American Resource Guide, A. Diggs
The African American Address Book, J. Crayton
The Secrets of Savvy Networking, S. Roane
Success Runs in Our Race, G. Frazer

About Computers

Macs for Dummies, D. Pogue
PC's for Dummies, D. Gookin
The Internet for Dummies, R. Levine

About Enjoyment

Makes Me Wanna Holler, N. McCall
Five Minutes to Midnight, R. Lapchick
The Fire Next Time, J. Baldwin
I Know Why the Caged Bird Sings,
   M. Angelou

About History

African Presence in World Culture,
   I. Sertima
Stolen Legacy, G. James
Two Nations, A. Hacker
Black Man of Nile, Y. Ben-Jochannan

About Inspiration

Acts of Faith, I. Vanzant
Children of the Dream, A. Edwards
Live Your Dreams, L. Brown
Think and Grow Rich, D. Kimbro

About People

Autobiography of Malcolm X, A. Haley
Autobiography of W.E.B. DuBois
Autobiography of Martin Luther King
The Story of Marcus Garvey, E. Cronon

BACK COURT

Food For Thought

Excerpts from Players Past

Intro: What are the Issues?

Herb Crosby

Position: Guard; **College:** Univ. of Okla.; **Degree:** BS Biology; **Masters:** S. Calif. College of Chiropractic; **Current Status:** Chiropractic doctor; **Career Highlights:** Graduated from the Univ. of Oklahoma in 1986 with a degree in Biology and from S. Calif. College of Chiropractic with a Masters in Chiropractic's in 1990. Scored 35 points in a game as a sophomore.

Intro: Like many young men, I had played basketball with dreams of becoming a professional athlete. However, there came a time in my life when I had to make a realistic decision on what path to choose. I chose education, and I now have a flourishing Chiropractic practice. If you were to choose education first and foremost, career success is certain. The fact is that more people benefit longer from an education, as opposed to a sports career. Remember: You are a ***student first*** and an ***athlete second.***

CHAP. 1: WAKE UP!

Anthony Davis

Position: Tailback **College:** USC **Major:** Speech Communication **Current Status:** Managing Partner-Casden Partners, Spokesperson for Nike, Miraval Resorts and The Greatest Moments. **Career Highlights:** 6 touchdown performance vs Notre Dame in '72, NCAA record for kickoff returns for touchdowns (6). Two sport All-American (baseball & football) and 4 National Titles.

Intro: I came from a socio-economically depressed area, and I learned at an early age that I had to focus on academics in order to realize my potential in sports. Often times white athletes are more prepared for life outside of sports than we are. We tend to think "If I can throw the ball or can dunk, then I am going to the pros." But the pros don't last forever. If you want to be successful then find someone to give you academic guidance and raise your awareness. My mentors were Bobby Rogers, Edussell Garrison and Charles Young. Much gratitude. Remember: *The Cream <u>always</u> rises to the top.*

Kenny Smith

Position: Guard **College:** UNC **Major:** LS&A **Current Status:** NBA- Houston Rockets
Career Highlights: Two World Championships with the Houston Rockets.

Intro: The biggest thing that I looked at when selecting a school was to see if it offered a balanced environment (i.e., good academics, good basketball and a social life). I visited Duke, the University of Virginia, St. Johns, and my eventual alma mater North Carolina. I chose UNC for a number of reasons: (1) Good academic and athletic records of success. (2) The stability of the coaching staff and Coach Dean Smith. (3) The success of former players and graduates of the school, and their positive comments about UNC. (4) I felt it would give me the greatest opportunity to be successful in life after basketball. These aspects are immeasurable in your career. Everyone doesn't make it in the NBA, so choosing a school which gives you the greatest opportunity for success both on and off the court is your best bet.

Bob Lanier

Position: Center **College:** St. Bonaventure **Degree:** Business Administration, Honor-ary Doctorate **Current Status:** President- Bob Lanier Enterprises **Career Highlights:** Played 14 years in the NBA.

Intro: In preparation for college, you must focus on the academic challenge that it presents, as well as the amount of playing time and recognition you may or may not receive. Your first year will be your most difficult in adjusting on campus, mainly because of the im-personal atmosphere in the larger classes. Note taking skills are a must, because you can't write fast enough to get everything. Preparation and making quick adjustments were key reasons why <u>I was able to graduate in four years</u>, which rarely happens at all anymore. With the right approach, you can do the same. Good luck in your endeavors!

Vince Albritton

Position: Safety **College:** Univ. of Washington **Major:** Speech Communication
Current Status: Retired from the NFL, currently preparing to work for the Dallas Fire Department. **Career Highlights:** Played on two Rose Bowl teams and played for the Dallas Cowboys (1985-1992)

Intro: My college experience was fairly positive in meeting different types of people, but there were some very difficult periods of adjustment with regards to the social and academic life. I did have my share of problems adjusting to college life. As a freshman I had this sociology class where the instructor asked us the first day, "How many ball players do I have in my class?" After we responded in numbers, he said

"My class requires serious academic performance, so I suggest you find another class to sit in on." One of my few mentors was Dr. Jones, a speech professor who expressed to me the importance of being articulate. I already commanded the attention of my audience by my presence, but he helped me polish my presentation skills. His encouragement helped make the transition easier.

CHAP. 5: ROAD WORK

Marvin Cobb

Position: Outside Linebacker **College:** USC **Degree:** B.A. Business Mgmt 1975 **Current Status:** Director of the USC School of Medicine- Independent Provider Association **Career Highlights:** Carried 20 units his last semester in order to graduate in four years. Stole a base and scored the winning run in the 1973 College World Series.

Intro: As a former Director of Academics at USC, my advice is as follows: There are basically two lies that I saw being perpetrated on young student-athletes: 1) The dumb jock syndrome, which means that to be athletically superior you must be academically inferior. 2) The things that are taught in the classroom are not important to everyday life, so you have no practical need for the information. Hard work, discipline, dedication and focus are all traits that can be used as tools for success in an academic setting. School serves as a practice field for life skills. Just as in football, you don't just show up in the real world without preparation and practice. Like many schools, USC knowingly enroll athletes that cannot function on a college level. They promise the student-athletes and their parents that they are going to provide them with an education, when in reality they are often setting them up for failure. No matter what they promise, _it is up to you_ to make it happen in order to avoid being exploited.

CHAP. 6: SMARTER NOT HARDER

Gerald Irons

Position: Linebacker **College:** University of Maryland Eastern Shore **Degree:** Business Administration **Masters:** University of Chicago Business School **Current Status:** Director of Business Development-The Woodlands, Inc., and President of Conroe School District. **Career Highlights:** Oakland Raiders and Cleveland Browns from 1971-1980.

Intro: Being a focused person enables me to do more than one thing at a time. I knew that football would demand a lot of my time, as would academics. The equilibrium between sports and academics must be maintained. The following tips can greatly enhance your study skills: (1) Distinguish between dreams and goals, and write out a plan for achievement. (2) Tap into the large number of resources available to you. (3) Work to develop good listening skills: we have two eyes and ears thus the importance of retention. (4) Take good copious notes, develop a personal short hand, and transcribe them ASAP. (5) Talk to your professors, and show an active interest in your academics. (6) Meditation: I practice Psycho-Cybernetics daily, to visualize the realization and completion of tasks. Be motivated enough to become innovative in achieving your academic goals. I attended the University of Chicago business school, and took two extra courses (both of which met on the same day at the same time). I sat in on the first half of one, and the second half of the other for the entire quarter, and passed both in order to graduate that spring. You can make a way, where there is no way.

CHAP. 7: WORKING THE CLOCK

Johnny Newman

Position: Guard **College:** Univ. of Richmond **Degree:** Criminal Justice & Political Science **Current Status:** Guard- Milwaukee Bucks **Career Highlights:** Double major and still graduated in four years. Ten year NBA career with the N.Y. Knicks, Charlotte Hornets and Milwaukee Bucks.

Intro: Time management is one of the greatest attributes that a student-athlete can develop, one that will help you long after your college career is over. If your time is managed properly, you will be able to accomplish a lot more than most people. I used this skill to receive a dual degree, and to free up more time for social interaction, an important aspect of the college experience. If you put your priorities in order, then you will develop tremendous life skills that you can carry with you. Kids today need to understand what is really going on, and realize that these skills are going to put food on your table and keep clothing on your back for the duration of your life. So if you don't possess time management skills, you need to start developing them. Your future depends on it.

CHAP. 8: POLITICS AND PLAYING TIME

Stacy Robinson

Position: Wide Receiver **College:** N. Dakota State **Degree:** BA, MBA Fairleigh Dickinson University **Current Status:** Director of Player Development-NFLPA.
Career Highlights: Masters Degree completed while winning two Super Bowls with the N.Y. Giants.

Intro: One thing I remember *(as an African American male at an all white college)* is the perception of my coaches that I was un-disciplined. The coaches' concerns were based upon cultural differences. My greatest learning experience came at the pro level under Bill Parcells, then head coach of the New York Giants. There was friction from day one. I got hurt during the strike-shortened 1987 season, and when I returned I was relegated to fifth string. The next season I was released, brought back the fifth week and earned a starting spot the rest of the way. This cycle repeated itself for the next two years. One season I was kept out of a playoff game in favor of a rookie, who was cramming to learn both receiver positions the morning of the game. I was livid and I took this one personally. There were times when I wanted to knock him out, but

I was able to check my emotions at the door. *Remember:* Although you might not like or respect the coach, always have respect for the position.

CHAP. 9: MONEY MATTERS
Kevin Steward

Position: Guard **College:** USC **Degree:** BS Public Administration **Current Status:** Mortgage Banker **Career Highlights:** Four time member of University of Southern California Deans List. High School BCI tournament All-American.

Intro: Young people need to be disciplined with regards to their money and credit. In terms of paying bills, if you do not know how to manage your money you should look to a close relative or friend for assistance. Young people must realize that the so called "free ride" does not last forever, and financial planning helps you get ready for the real world. The key points to remember when it comes to finance are: (1) Build and maintain your credit, it will follow you around for the rest of your life. (2) Don't try to be larger than you are. (3) Don't jeopardize your scholarship by doing petty crimes or hustles to make a few bucks. (4) Develop a monthly budget or plan, know your limitations and live according to them. Put these principles into practice, and you will be able to stretch your money a little further.

CHAP. 10: THE ART OF NETWORKING
Kent Hill

Position: Off. Line **College:** Georgia Tech **Degree:** BA Industrial Management **Current Status:** Assistant Athletic Director, Georgia Tech. **Career Highlights:** First round draft pick by the Los Angeles Rams in 1979, Super Bowl starter as a rookie, and three time All Pro.

Intro: Networking is such an important tool in the successful development of your life and career. Far too often this area is neglected by the student-athlete at a time when his/her opportunities are greatest. It is important that you make a positive impression on everyone you meet during your career. This will help to develop that contact into a valuable resource, thus creating more career options for yourself after college. I am extremely pleased to see that the authors have included this topic in the book.

CHAP. 11: FEMALES
Earvin "Magic" Johnson

Position: Guard **College:** Michigan State **Current Status:** President- Magic Johnson Enterprises **Career Highlights:** First round draft pick by the Los Angeles Lakers in 1979, five world championships, three league MVP awards and one Olympic gold medal.
Intro: Sexual desire is perfectly natural, and sexual fulfillment is a very important part of most people's lives. The challenge we all face is to learn how to express our sexuality in ways that respect others as well as ourselves. And now, in the age of

AIDS, the challenge is even greater, for we have to learn how to express our sexuality and gratify our desires in ways that don't risk the health of others or ourselves. If you're considering becoming sexually active, you should ask yourself the following questions: (1) Am I prepared to practice safer sex each and every time I have sex? (2) Am I prepared to use contraception each and every time I have man-woman sex? (3) Am I prepared to deal with the consequences if I or my partner(s) become infected with HIV or another STD or become pregnant? (4) Am I prepared to say no when I think it's not right for me? If you say yes to these questions while you're still a teenager, I have to ask, "Are you sure?"[1]

CHAP. 12: ALMOST ADDICTED

Reggie Rogers

Position: Def. Line **College:** Univ. of Washington **Major:** Sociology **Current Status:** CFL **Career Highlights:** First Team All-American in 1988, and a first round draft pick of the Detroit Lions in the same year.

Intro: It hit me like a ton of bricks, when I lost my brother Don to a cocaine-induced heart attack. Don was a square growing up, and when he got to UCLA, he started trying to get a little hip. The worst thing for him was getting caught up with teammates who were drug users. Alcohol was a way for me to deal with the depression of Don's death, because that is how I had always dealt with my problems. At my house we didn't just come home talking about our problems like *Leave it to Beaver*, we just hung out and drank. As a result of my drinking I ended up having a serious car accident where three teenagers died. This changed my life and the lives of three other families. If I had to do it all over again I would never turn to a bottle for any answers to life's questions. My advice: "Man, leave that shit alone. It will mess up your life."

CHAP. 13: MEDIA RELATIONS

Harry Carson

Position: Linebacker **College:** S. Carolina St. **Degree:** BA Communications **Current Status:** Broadcast Journalist **Career Highlights:** Played linebacker for the New York Giants for 13 years. Six Pro Bowl appearances and two Super Bowl Championships. **Intro:** Let me start out by saying that every chapter of this book contains valuable and useful information for the African-American student-athlete. In regards to media relations, throughout my athletic career I enjoyed my relationship with the media. I understood that those reporters covering football had a job to do. I grew to understand that those in the media could care less about me as an individual. Their job is to sell papers and we all know that negative press sells better and faster than positive press. When giving an interview think very carefully about what you say before it comes out of your mouth. Project yourself using correct grammar instead of the "you knows" or the "you know what I mean" phrases that we often hear. This will speak volumes about you as an individual, but also of the people who've labored to get you where you are today.

Kellen Winslow

Position: Tight End **College:** Univ. of Missouri **Degree:** BES Counseling Psychology, J.D. Univ. of San Diego **Current Status:** V.P. of Football Operations for Precept Sports and President of the African American Sports Foundation. **Career Highlights:** All Big-Eight academic team, and earning a JD. Five Time All-Pro and a member of the NFL Hall of Fame.

Intro: Today, many qualified African American agents are kept out of the loop in terms of obtaining clients, for a myriad of reasons, one being that our people have been conditioned to believe that because someone is white, they are automatically qualified. Brothers who may be equal or superior in education are often made to jump through hoops to prove themselves worthy of an athlete's business. This brainwashing is an affirmation of racial self-hatred, and leads to a lack of investment in our communities as a whole. A good agent will act as mentor, play an active role in your personal development and involve you in the development of your community. Above all, you must play an active role in your personal development. Surround yourself with positive people who possess a general love and concern for you as well as your people. Follow these criteria, and you can't help but make the right decision.

ABOUT CULTURE

Jimmy Jackson

Position: Guard **College:** Ohio State University **Major:** Business **Status:** NBA Guard-Dallas Mavericks **Career Highlights:** Currently completing classes at OSU to get degree in business. Won the Big Ten championship sophomore year (1990-91).

Intro: I remember how much of a drastic change college was for me, in that I came from the pre-dominantly African-American *Macomber Vocational School* in Toledo, Ohio. At OSU, you had 58,000 students on campus, and only 2,500 were African-American. I felt a strong need to build and maintain cultural ties, and to become more knowledgeable about my history. Fortunately for me we had the Frank Hale Cultural Center, a center where were we got together for Afro-centric study and dialogue. My development as an African-American male made campus life a lot easier. Knowledge of self and high self-esteem helped me keep everything in perspective with regards to my status as a student-athlete. Remember: *knowing who you are* is half the battle.

[1] *What you can do to avoid AIDS*, by Earvin Magic Johnson, Copyright 1992-*Times Books*

Easy-Index

Footnotes

---

[1] V. Blossom, *It Has Happened,* 1959

[2] A. Edwards & G. Polite, *Children of the Dream,* 1993

[3] A. Hacker, *Two Nations,* 1995

[4] "Playing ball with colleges." USA Weekend. Jan. 21-23 1994

[5] Henry L. Gates, Jr., Harvard University

[6] Drake Beam Morin Career Transition Study

[6] Ibid

[7] T. Strecker, *The Strecker Memorandum,* 1986

[8] *Sports Illustrated,* April 3, 1995, "Was the X factor a factor?"

[9] K. Shropshire-Associate Professor of Legal Studies at the Wharton School of the University of Pennsylvania

[10] *Negotiating The Deals.* Black Enterprise. July 1995. Vol. 25, No. 12

[11] Ibid

[12] *Sociology,* John M. Shepard-Univ. of Kentucky

[13] *Sociology,* John M. Shepard-Univ. of Kentucky

PLAYER PROFILES

Authors' Biographical Sketch

37 Vince Fudzie

Vince was raised in a West Oakland neighborhood, riddled with drugs, violence and prostitution, where he lived with his mother and three sisters. Vince is a product of an environment which included a deteriorating public school system. Despite the fact that Vince was considered for special education in the second grade because of his inability to read, he went on to excel in school. Astonishingly, his high school counselor attempted to limit his potential by telling him that he lacked the intelligence to succeed in college, even though he had a stellar GPA. However, with perseverance, Vince entered the University of Washington on a football scholarship. Although Vince struggled with many of these issues, he quickly learned to manage the dual role of student and major college athlete. Vince went on to receive a B.A. in Business Administration from the University of Washington and a M.B.A. from the University of Michigan.

18 Andre Hayes

Andre grew up in a single parent home in a South Central Los Angeles neighborhood. In his mother's attempt to shelter him from the harsh realities of his environment, she struggled and sacrificed to send him to parochial schools every year of his pre-college education. In the fall of 1981, Andre entered the University of Washington, where he quickly discovered the rigors of being a student-athlete. As a result of his being ill-prepared to deal with these rigors, he subsequently flunked out of school (on two separate occasions) and was forced to attend junior college before he could be reinstated. It was during his stint at Seattle Central that he finally realized the tremendous educational opportunity he was wasting. Andre went on to improve his academic record and eventually graduate from the University of Washington with a degree in Criminal Justice. He is currently teaching Social Science at his high school alma mater.

notes:

notes:

notes:

notes:

notes: